Solutions Manual to Accompany

JOHNSTON • DiNARDO

ECONOMETRIC METHODS

Fourth Edition

HIROYUKI KAWAKATSU

University of California - Irvine

The McGraw-Hill Companies, Inc.
New York St. Louis San Francisco Auckland Bogotá
Caracas Lisbon London Madrid Mexico City Milan Montreal
New Delhi San Juan Singapore Sydney Tokyo Toronto

McGraw-Hill

*A Division of The **McGraw·Hill** Companies*

Solutions Manual to Accompany
ECONOMETRIC METHODS Fourth Edition

ISBN 0-07-032723-8

4 5 6 7 8 9 0 GDP GDP 0 9 8 7 6 5 4 3 2 1

http://www.mhcollege.com

Contents

Chapter 1

1.1. One can measure volatility by the sample variance or by the sample standard deviation. However, these measures of volatility depend on the unit of measurement and are not suited to compare volatility of two series that are measured in different units. The coefficient of variation, as defined in the text, is a normalized unit-free measure of volatility that can be used for comparison. Summary statistics of the three series (savings, income, and the savings ratio) are

Variable	Obs	Mean	Std. Dev.	Min	Max
inc	133	2403.795	711.715	1267.7	3579.9
sav	133	162.2343	50.50461	71.15714	266.3042
sav/inc	133	.068608	.0142615	.0305521	.1066919

The coefficient of variation of the three series are

$$
\begin{aligned}
INC &= 711.715/2403.795 \times 100 &= 29.61 \\
SAV &= 50.50461/162.2343 \times 100 &= 31.13 \\
SAV/INC &= .0142615/.068608 \times 100 &= 20.79
\end{aligned}
$$

Although income "looks" much less volatile than savings in Fig. 1.1a, the two series do not have a much different coefficient of variation. The savings ratio is less volatile than either savings or income.

1.2. For example, the first entry in the first row 66.31, which is the conditional mean of Height given that Chest is 33–35, can be computed as

$$
\begin{aligned}
E(H \mid C_j) &= \sum_i H_i \Pr(H_i \mid C_j) \\
&= 64.5 \times \frac{39}{103} + 66.5 \times \frac{40}{103} + 68.5 \times \frac{19}{103} + 70.5 \times \frac{5}{103} + 72.5 \times \frac{0}{103} \\
&= 66.31
\end{aligned}
$$

The last entry in the second row 41.80, which is the conditional mean of Chest given that Height is 72–73, can be computed as

$$
\begin{aligned}
E(C \mid H_j) &= \sum_i C_i \Pr(C_i \mid H_j) \\
&= 34 \times \frac{0}{317} + 37 \times \frac{17}{317} + 40 \times \frac{120}{317} + 43 \times \frac{153}{317} + 46.5 \times \frac{27}{317} \\
&= 41.84
\end{aligned}
$$

Similary for other entries.

1.3. The second expression follows from substituting $s_x = \sqrt{\sum x^2/n}$, $s_y = \sqrt{\sum y^2/n}$ into the first expression

$$
\begin{aligned}
r &= \frac{\sum xy}{n s_x s_y} \\
&= \frac{\sum xy}{n\sqrt{\sum x^2/n}\sqrt{\sum y^2/n}} \\
&= \frac{\sum xy}{\sqrt{\sum x^2}\sqrt{\sum y^2}}
\end{aligned}
$$

The third expression follows from using the definition

$$
\begin{aligned}
x &= X - \overline{X} &= X - \sum X/n \\
y &= Y - \overline{Y} &= Y - \sum Y/n
\end{aligned}
$$

Then

$$
\begin{aligned}
\sum xy &= \sum (X - \overline{X})(Y - \overline{Y}) \\
&= \sum (XY - X\overline{Y} - \overline{X}Y + \overline{XY}) \\
&= \sum XY - \overline{Y}\sum X - \overline{X}\sum Y + n\overline{XY} \\
&= \sum XY - \frac{\sum Y}{n}\sum X - \frac{\sum X}{n}\sum Y + n\frac{\sum X}{n}\frac{\sum Y}{n} \\
&= \sum XY - \frac{\sum X \sum Y}{n}
\end{aligned}
$$

$$
\begin{aligned}
\sum x^2 &= \sum (X - \overline{X})^2 \\
&= \sum (X^2 - 2X\overline{X} + \overline{X}^2) \\
&= \sum X^2 - 2\overline{X}\sum X + n\overline{X}^2 \\
&= \sum X^2 - 2\frac{\sum X}{n}\sum X + n\left(\frac{\sum X}{n}\right)^2 \\
&= \sum X^2 - \frac{(\sum X)^2}{n}
\end{aligned}
$$

and

$$
\sum y^2 = \sum Y^2 - \frac{(\sum Y)^2}{n}
$$

Therefore

$$
\begin{aligned}
\frac{\sum xy}{\sqrt{\sum x^2}\sqrt{\sum y^2}} &= \frac{\sum XY - \sum X \sum Y/n}{\sqrt{\sum X^2 - (\sum X)^2/n}\sqrt{\sum Y^2 - (\sum Y)^2/n}} \\
&= \frac{n\sum XY - \sum X \sum Y}{\sqrt{n\sum X^2 - (\sum X)^2}\sqrt{n\sum Y^2 - (\sum Y)^2}}
\end{aligned}
$$

1.4. You just crank out the tedious algebra.

$$
\begin{aligned}
f(y \mid x) &= f(x,y)/f(x) \\
&= \frac{1}{\sqrt{2\pi}\sigma_y\sqrt{1-\rho^2}} \exp\left\{ -\frac{1}{2(1-\rho^2)}\left[\left(\frac{y-\mu_y}{\sigma_y}\right)^2 - 2\rho\left(\frac{x-\mu_x}{\sigma_x}\right)\left(\frac{y-\mu_y}{\sigma_y}\right) \right.\right. \\
&\qquad \left.\left. + \left(\frac{x-\mu_x}{\sigma_x}\right)^2 \right] + \frac{1}{2}\left(\frac{x-\mu_x}{\sigma_x}\right)^2 \right\} \\
&= \frac{1}{\sqrt{2\pi}\sigma_y\sqrt{1-\rho^2}} \exp\left\{ -\frac{1}{2}\left[\frac{y - \left(\mu_y - \rho\frac{\sigma_y}{\sigma_x}\mu_x + \rho\frac{\sigma_y}{\sigma_y}x\right)}{\sigma_y\sqrt{1-\rho^2}} \right]^2 \right\}
\end{aligned}
$$

where

$$
\sigma_{y|x} = \sigma_y\sqrt{1-\rho^2}, \qquad \alpha = \mu_y - \rho\frac{\sigma_y}{\sigma_x}\mu_x, \qquad \beta = \rho\frac{\sigma_y}{\sigma_x}.
$$

1.5.

Sample	Correlation
59.1–92.1	−0.023725
59.1–73.3	−0.923373
73.4–81.4	−0.891777
82.1–92.1	−0.751723

1.6. The results from fitting to the whole sample gives

```
============================================================
LS // Dependent Variable is GAS
Sample: 1959:1 1992:1
Included observations: 133
============================================================
     Variable      CoefficienStd. Errort-Statistic  Prob.
============================================================
        C          -7.681375  0.297338  -25.83381   0.0000
      PRICE        -0.017098  0.062950  -0.271618    0.7863
============================================================
R-squared              0.000563   Mean dependent var-7.762089
Adjusted R-squared    -0.007066   S.D. dependent var 0.117997
S.E. of regression     0.118413   Akaike info criter-4.252222
Sum squared resid      1.836850   Schwarz criterion -4.208758
Log likelihood        96.05394    F-statistic        0.073777
Durbin-Watson stat     0.024600   Prob(F-statistic)  0.786343
============================================================
```

There does not appear to be any linear relation between gasoline consumption and price; the R^2 is almost zero and the coefficient on price is not significant.

1.7.

(*a*) With replacement

		Y		
		1	2	3
	1	1/9	1/9	1/9
X	2	1/9	1/9	1/9
	3	1/9	1/9	1/9

Since the draw is random, the probability of choosing any number on the first draw is 1/3. With replacement, the probability of choosing any number on the second draw is also 1/3. Since the two draws are independent, the joint probability of choosing any pair of numbers is $1/3 \times 1/3 = 1/9$.

The marginal distribution of X is

$$f(X_i) = \sum_j f(X_i, Y_j) = \frac{1}{3} \qquad \text{for } X_i = 1, 2, 3.$$

and the unconditional mean of X is

$$\mu_x = E(X) = \sum_i X_i f(X_i) = 2$$

Since the distribution is symmetric in X and Y (see the table), the same result holds for Y. The conditional mean of X given Y is

$$E(X \mid Y_j) = \sum_i X_i f(X_i \mid Y_j) = \sum_i X_i \frac{f(X_i, Y_j)}{f(Y_j)} = \frac{1 + 2 + 3}{3} = 2 \qquad \text{for } Y_j = 1, 2, 3.$$

The covariance between X and Y is

$$\sigma_{XY} = E(X - \mu_x)(Y - \mu_Y) = \sum_{i,j} f(X_i, Y_j)(X_i - 2)(Y_j - 2) = 0$$

so the correlation coefficient is 0.

(*b*) Without replacement

		Y		
		1	2	3
	1	0	1/6	1/6
X	2	1/6	0	1/6
	3	1/6	1/6	0

Without replacement it is impossible to draw the same number twice. The probability of drawing any pair of different numbers can be calculated as follows. The probability of chosing any number on the first draw is still 1/3. Out of the remaining two balls, the probability of choosing any different number on the second draw is 1/2. Therefore the joint probability of choosing a pair of different numbers is $1/3 \times 1/2 = 1/6$. Notice again that the distribution is symmetric in X and Y.

The marginal distribution of X is $f(X_i) = 1/3$ for $X_i = 1, 2, 3$ and the unconditional mean is $\mu_x = 2$; the same for Y from symmetry.

The conditional means of X given Y are

$$E(X \mid Y_j = 1) = 1 \times \frac{0}{6} + 2 \times \frac{3}{6} + 3 \times \frac{3}{6} = \frac{5}{2}$$

$$E(X \mid Y_j = 2) = 1 \times \frac{3}{6} + 2 \times \frac{0}{6} + 3 \times \frac{3}{6} = 2$$

$$E(X \mid Y_j = 3) = 1 \times \frac{3}{6} + 2 \times \frac{3}{6} + 3 \times \frac{0}{6} = \frac{3}{2}$$

The results are intuitive: given that your second draw is a big number, you expect to have chosen a small number on the first draw and vice versa. Therefore we expect X and Y to be negatively correlated.

The covariance between X and Y is $\sigma_{XY} = -1/3$ and the variance of X (or Y) is $\sigma_X^2 = \sigma_Y^2 = 2/3$. The correlation coefficient is

$$\rho = \frac{\sigma_{XY}}{\sigma_X \sigma_Y} = -\frac{1}{2}$$

1.8.

		Y	
		2	5
X	1	.2	.3
	3	.1	.4

For example

$$
\begin{aligned}
f(X_i = 1, Y_j = 2) &= \sum_k f(X_i, Y_j, Z_k) \\
&= f(1, 2, 4) + f(1, 2, 8) \\
&= .2
\end{aligned}
$$

and similar for other entries.

1.9.   First we verify that the u's have zero mean and zero covariance. The marginal distributions are

$$
\begin{aligned}
f(u_1) &= 0.5 \quad \text{for } u_1 = -1, 1 \\
f(u_2) &= 0.5 \quad \text{for } u_2 = -2, 2
\end{aligned}
$$

Therefore the means of u_1, u_2 are

$$
\begin{aligned}
E(u_1) &= -1 \times .5 + 1 \times .5 = 0 \\
E(u_2) &= -2 \times .5 + 2 \times .5 = 0
\end{aligned}
$$

and the covariance is

$$\sigma_{12} = E(u_1 u_2) = \sum u_1 u_2 f(u_1, u_2) = 0$$

To derive the sampling distribution of b, we rewrite it in terms of the u's as

$$
\begin{aligned}
b &= \frac{\sum XY}{\sum X^2} = \frac{\sum X(\beta X + u)}{\sum X^2} \\
&= \beta + \frac{\sum Xu}{\sum X^2} = \beta + \frac{u_1 + 2u_2}{5}
\end{aligned}
$$

From the joint distribution of u's, we see that $u_1 + 2u_2$ takes the values $-5, -3, 3, 5$, each with equal probability .25. Therefore

$$
E(b) = \beta
$$

and

$$
\begin{aligned}
var(b) &= E\left(\frac{u_1 + 2u_2}{5}\right)^2 \\
&= \frac{1}{25} \times \frac{(-5)^2 + (-3)^2 + 3^2 + 5^2}{4} \\
&= .68
\end{aligned}
$$

1.10.   The postulated relation is

$$
Y_i = \alpha + \beta X_i + u_i \qquad \text{where } u \sim iid(0, \sigma^2).
$$

Then

$$
\begin{aligned}
b &= \frac{1}{8}(Y_6 + Y_5 - Y_2 - Y_1) \\
&= \frac{1}{8}\left(\alpha + 6\beta + u_6 + \alpha + 5\beta + u_5 - (\alpha + 2\beta + u_2) - (\alpha + \beta + u_1)\right) \\
&= \beta + \frac{1}{8}(u_6 + u_5 - u_2 - u_1)
\end{aligned}
$$

Taking expectations we have

$$
E(b) = \beta \qquad \text{and} \qquad var(b) = \frac{4}{64}\sigma^2 = \frac{1}{16}\sigma^2
$$

The variance of the OLS estimator is

$$
var(b_{OLS}) = \frac{\sigma^2}{\sum x^2} = \frac{2}{35}\sigma^2
$$

Since b is a linear unbiased estimator we know from the Gauss-Markov theorem that its variance cannot be larger than that of OLS. The efficiency of b is

$$
\frac{var(b_{OLS})}{var(b)} = \frac{32}{35} = .914
$$

which is not so bad for this sample.

1.11.   The r^2 from the regression of X on Y is be the variation in X that is explained (linearly) by Y. Note well that this does not have any causal interpretation.

$$
b_{yx}b_{xy} = \frac{\sum xy}{\sum x^2}\frac{\sum yx}{\sum y^2} = \frac{(\sum xy)^2}{\sum x^2 \sum y^2} = r^2 \leq 1
$$

where the last inequality follows from the Cauchy-Schwarz inequality.

With Y on the vertical axis, the regression of Y on X has slope b_{yx} and the regression of X on Y has slope $1/b_{xy}$. Since b_{xy} and b_{yx} have the same sign we can divide both sides of the inequality by $|b_{xy}|$ and write

$$|b_{yx}| \leq \left| \frac{1}{b_{xy}} \right|$$

The *absolute value* of the slope from regressing Y on X is always smaller than that from regressing X on Y.

For the numerical example we have

$$\sum xy = \sum (X - \overline{X})(Y - \overline{Y}) = \sum XY - n\overline{XY} = 20.955$$

$$\sum x^2 = \sum X^2 - n\overline{X}^2 = 11.517$$

$$\sum y^2 = \sum Y^2 - n\overline{Y}^2 = 82.813$$

so that

$$b_{yx} = \frac{\sum xy}{\sum x^2} = 1.819$$

$$b_{xy} = \frac{\sum xy}{\sum y^2} = .253$$

$$r^2 = \frac{(\sum xy)^2}{\sum x^2 \sum y^2} = .460$$

This confirms

$$b_{yx} b_{xy} = .460 = r^2 \qquad \text{and} \qquad b_{yx} = 1.819 < 3.953 = \frac{1}{b_{xy}}$$

1.12.   Let

$$X' = aX + b, \quad Y' = cY + d, \quad r' = corr(X', Y').$$

We want to show $r'^2 = r^2$. The key step is to notice that

$$x' = X' - \overline{X'} = aX + b - (a\overline{X} + b) = a(X - \overline{X}) = ax$$
$$y' = Y' - \overline{Y'} = cY + d - (c\overline{Y} + d) = c(Y - \overline{Y}) = cy$$

Then

$$r'^2 = \frac{(\sum x'y')^2}{\sum x'^2 \sum y'^2} = \frac{(\sum ax \cdot cy)^2}{\sum (ax)^2 \sum (cy)^2} = \frac{(\sum xy)^2}{\sum x^2 \sum y^2} = r^2$$

This shows that the *squared* correlation coefficient is scale-location invariant. (This is not true for r; if $ac > 0$ then $r' = r$ but if $ac < 0$ then $r' = -r$.)

1.13.   Applying the OLS formula to the two regressions, we have

$$1.2 = \sum yc / \sum c^2$$
$$0.6 = \sum yc / \sum y^2$$

or

$$\sum c^2 \;=\; \sum yc/1.2 \tag{1.1}$$

$$\sum y^2 \;=\; \sum yc/0.6 \tag{1.2}$$

(Notice that $\sum yc > 0$. This will be used in calculating the correlations.)

We also have the identity $Y = C + Z$. Taking the mean and subtracting, this identity also holds in deviation form $y = c + z$. My strategy is to express all quantities in terms of $\sum yc$ using (1.1) and (1.2). Thus

$$\sum z^2 = \sum (y - c)^2 = \sum y^2 - 2\sum yc + \sum c^2 = \frac{1}{2}\sum yc$$

$$\sum yz = \sum y(y - c) = \sum y^2 - \sum yc = \frac{2}{3}\sum yc$$

$$\sum cz = \sum c(y - c) = \sum yc - \sum c^2 = \frac{1}{6}\sum yc$$

so that

$$r_{YZ} = \frac{\sum yz}{\sqrt{\sum y^2}\sqrt{\sum z^2}} = \frac{\frac{2}{3}\sum yc}{\sqrt{\frac{1}{0.6}\sum yc}\sqrt{\frac{1}{2}\sum yc}} = \sqrt{\frac{8}{15}} = .730$$

$$r_{cz} = \frac{\sum cz}{\sqrt{\sum c^2}\sqrt{\sum z^2}} = \frac{\frac{1}{6}\sum yc}{\sqrt{\frac{1}{1.2}\sum yc}\sqrt{\frac{1}{2}\sum yc}} = \sqrt{\frac{1}{15}} = .258$$

$$\frac{s_Z}{s_Y} = \sqrt{\frac{\sum z^2}{\sum y^2}} = \sqrt{0.3} = .548$$

1.14.   It is true that (subscripts refer to the subsamples)

$$\sum X^2 = \sum_1 X^2 + \sum_2 X^2, \qquad \sum XY = \sum_1 XY + \sum_2 XY$$

but

$$\sum x^2 = \sum_1 x^2 + \sum_2 x^2, \qquad \sum xy = \sum_1 xy + \sum_2 xy$$

do *not* hold in general. This is so because the two sub-samples do not have the same mean; this is why the overall correlation can be smaller than either correlations in the subsamples. Therefore we use the last formula in Eq. (1.3)

$$r = \frac{n\sum XY - \sum X \sum Y}{\sqrt{n\sum X^2 - (\sum X)^2}\sqrt{n\sum Y^2 - (\sum Y)^2}}$$

First,

$$\sum X = \sum_1 X + \sum_2 X = n_1\overline{X}_1 + n_2\overline{X}_2 = 5800$$

$$\sum Y = \sum_1 Y + \sum_2 Y = n_1\overline{Y}_1 + n_2\overline{Y}_2 = 11200$$

Next, from

$$s_x^2 = \frac{\sum x^2}{n} = \frac{\sum X^2 - n\overline{X}^2}{n}$$

we can write

$$\sum X^2 = n(s_x^2 + \overline{X}^2)$$

Thus

$$\sum X^2 = \sum_1 X^2 + \sum_2 X^2 = n_1(s_{X_1}^2 + \overline{X}_1^2) + n_2(s_{X_2}^2 + \overline{X}_2^2) = 40600$$

$$\sum Y^2 = \sum_1 Y^2 + \sum_2 Y^2 = n_1(s_{Y_1}^2 + \overline{Y}_1^2) + n_2(s_{Y_2}^2 + \overline{Y}_2^2) = 138200$$

Finally, we calculate $\sum XY$. From the first formula in Eq. (1.3) we have

$$rns_X s_Y = \sum xy = \sum(X - \overline{X})(Y - \overline{Y}) = \sum XY - n\overline{XY}$$

which gives

$$\sum XY = n(rs_X s_Y + \overline{XY})$$

Thus

$$\begin{aligned}
\sum XY &= \sum_1 XY + \sum_2 XY \\
&= n_1(r_1 s_{X_1} s_{Y_1} + \overline{X_1 Y_1}) + n_2(r_2 s_{X_2} s_{Y_2} + \overline{X_2 Y_2}) \\
&= 69520
\end{aligned}$$

Putting these results together we get

$$\begin{aligned}
r &= \frac{n\sum XY - \sum X \sum Y}{\sqrt{n\sum X^2 - (\sum X)^2}\sqrt{n\sum Y^2 - (\sum Y)^2}} \\
&= \frac{6952 - 58 \times 112}{\sqrt{4060 - 58^2}\sqrt{13820 - 112^2}} \\
&= .484
\end{aligned}$$

1.15. Here is a sample session using stata.

```
. input X Y T

          X          Y          T
1.  60 23 35
2.  62 23 36
3.  61 25 37
4.  55 25 38
5.  53 26 39
6.  60 26 40
7.  63 29 41
8.  53 30 42
9.  52 30 43
10. 48 32 44
11. 49 33 45
```

```
12. 43 31 46
13. end

. corr, mean
(obs=12)
  Variable |        Mean    Std. Dev.        Min        Max
-----------+-----------------------------------------------------
         X |    54.91667     6.359793         43         63
         Y |       27.75       3.4935         23         33
         T |        40.5     3.605551         35         46


           |        X          Y          T
-----------+---------------------------
         X |   1.0000
         Y |  -0.7375     1.0000
         T |  -0.8068     0.9635     1.0000


. reg X T

    Source |       SS       df       MS                 Number of obs =      12
-----------+------------------------------             F(  1,    10) =   18.65
     Model |  289.596154     1   289.596154             Prob > F      =  0.0015
  Residual |  155.320513    10   15.5320513             R-square      =  0.6509
-----------+------------------------------             Adj R-square  =  0.6160
     Total |  444.916667    11   40.4469697             Root MSE      =  3.9411


------------------------------------------------------------------------------
         X |      Coef.   Std. Err.       t     P>|t|     [95% Conf. Interval]
-----------+------------------------------------------------------------------
         T |  -1.423077    .329569    -4.318    0.002    -2.157402   -.6887514
     _cons |   112.5513   13.39594     8.402    0.000     82.70326    142.3993
------------------------------------------------------------------------------

. pre resX, res

. reg Y T

    Source |       SS       df       MS                 Number of obs =      12
-----------+------------------------------             F(  1,    10) =  129.57
     Model |  124.631119     1   124.631119             Prob > F      =  0.0000
  Residual |  9.61888112    10   .961888112             R-square      =  0.9284
-----------+------------------------------             Adj R-square  =  0.9212
     Total |      134.25    11   12.2045455             Root MSE      =  .98076


------------------------------------------------------------------------------
         Y |      Coef.   Std. Err.       t     P>|t|     [95% Conf. Interval]
-----------+------------------------------------------------------------------
         T |   .9335664   .0820152    11.383    0.000     .7508252    1.116308
     _cons |  -10.05944   3.333659    -3.018    0.013     -17.4873   -2.631585
------------------------------------------------------------------------------
```

```
. pre resY, res

. corr resX resY Y
(obs=12)

        |    resX     resY       Y
--------+---------------------------
   resX|  1.0000
   resY|  0.2518   1.0000
      Y|  0.0674   0.2677   1.0000


. exit, clear
```

(*a*) The correlation between X and Y is $-.738$.

(*b*) (I depart from the notation in the text and denote the time trend as T and the deviation from mean of the time trend as $t = T - \overline{T}$.) Let $\widehat{X} = a_0 + b_0 T$ be the fitted values from the regression of X on trend T. Consider another trend variable $T' = \mu + \delta T$. μ depends on the choice of origin and δ depends on the unit of measurement. Let $\widetilde{X} = a_1 + b_1 T'$ be the fitted values from the regression of X on T'. We want to show $\widetilde{X} = \widehat{X}$.

Notice that

$$t' = T' - \overline{T'} = \mu + \delta T - (\mu + \delta \overline{T}) = \delta t$$

Therefore

$$b_1 = \frac{\sum xt'}{\sum t'^2} = \frac{\delta \sum xt}{\delta^2 \sum t^2} = \frac{b_0}{\delta}$$

and

$$\begin{aligned} a_1 &= \overline{X} - b_1 \overline{T'} = \overline{X} - \frac{b_0}{\delta}(\mu + \delta \overline{T}) \\ &= \overline{X} - b_0 \overline{T} - \frac{\mu}{\delta} b_0 = a_0 - \frac{\mu}{\delta} b_0 \end{aligned}$$

Then

$$\begin{aligned} \widetilde{X} &= a_1 + b_1 T' \\ &= a_0 - \frac{\mu}{\delta} b_0 + \frac{b_0}{\delta}(\mu + \delta T) \\ &= a_0 + b_0 T \\ &= \widehat{X} \end{aligned}$$

(*c*)

$$corr(e_{x,t}, Y) = .067 \quad \text{and} \quad corr(e_{x,t}, e_{y,t}) = .252$$

As can be seen from the regressions of X, Y on trend, both X and Y have significant trend components; X a negative trend and Y a positive trend. Therefore the seemingly high negative correlation between X and Y found in (*a*) seems to be driven by a common trend.

1.16.   From the OLS formula

$$b = \frac{\sum xy}{\sum x^2} = \frac{106.4}{215.4} = .494$$

$$a = \overline{Y} - b\overline{X} = \frac{21.9}{20} - .494 \times \frac{186.2}{20} = -3.504$$

To calculate the standard errors we first need an estimate of the error variance given in Eq. (1.31)

$$s^2 = \frac{\sum e^2}{n-2} = \frac{\sum y^2 - b^2 \sum x^2}{n-2} = \frac{1}{18}(86.9 - .494^2 \times 215.4) = 1.908$$

Then

$$s.e.(b) = \sqrt{\frac{s^2}{\sum x^2}} = \sqrt{\frac{1.908}{215.4}} = .094$$

$$s.e.(a) = \sqrt{s^2 \left(\frac{1}{n} + \frac{\overline{X}^2}{\sum x^2} \right)} = \sqrt{1.908 \left(\frac{1}{20} + \frac{9.31^2}{215.4} \right)} = .929$$

The conditional mean of Y given $X = 10$ is

$$E(Y \mid X = 10) = a + 10b = -3.504 + 10 \times .494 = 1.436$$

and the 95% confidence interval of this mean as given in Eq. (1.68) is

$$E(Y \mid X = 10) \pm t_{.975}(18)\sqrt{s^2 \left(\frac{1}{n} + \frac{(10 - \overline{X})^2}{\sum x^2} \right)}$$

$$= \quad 1.436 \pm 2.101\sqrt{1.908 \left(\frac{1}{20} + \frac{(10 - 9.31)^2}{215.4} \right)}$$

$$= \quad .773 \quad \text{to} \quad 2.099$$

Chapter 2

2.1.   I use two trend variables $T1 = YEAR - 1987$ and $T2 = YEAR - 1900$.

```
. input Y T1 T2

           Y        T1         T2
1. 38.1 -2 85
2. 80.0 -1 86
3. 170.4 0 87
4. 354.5 1 88
5. 744.4 2 89
6. end

. gen lnY=ln(Y)

. sum

Variable |     Obs        Mean    Std. Dev.        Min         Max
---------+-----------------------------------------------------------
       Y |       5      277.48    287.9729        38.1       744.4
      T1 |       5           0    1.581139          -2           2
      T2 |       5          87    1.581139          85          89
     lnY |       5    5.128735    1.175337    3.640214    6.612578

. reg lnY T1

    Source |       SS       df       MS              Number of obs =       5
-----------+------------------------------           F(  1,     3) =       .
     Model |  5.52555867    1  5.52555867           Prob > F      =  0.0000
  Residual |  .000113267    3  .000037756           R-square      =  1.0000
-----------+------------------------------           Adj R-square =  1.0000
     Total |  5.52567194    4  1.38141798           Root MSE      =  .00614

------------------------------------------------------------------------------
       lnY |      Coef.   Std. Err.        t    P>|t|     [95% Conf. Interval]
-----------+------------------------------------------------------------------
        T1 |    .743341   .0019431    382.557   0.000     .7371573    .7495248
     _cons |   5.128735   .0027479   1866.396   0.000      5.11999     5.13748
------------------------------------------------------------------------------

. reg lnY T2

    Source |       SS       df       MS              Number of obs =       5
-----------+------------------------------           F(  1,     3) =       .
     Model |  5.52555867    1  5.52555867           Prob > F      =  0.0000
  Residual |  .000113267    3  .000037756           R-square      =  1.0000
```

```
---------+---------------------------            Adj R-square  =   1.0000
  Total |  5.52567194   4  1.38141798            Root MSE      =    .00614

-----------------------------------------------------------------------------
   lnY |    Coef.   Std. Err.      t    P>|t|     [95% Conf. Interval]
-------+---------------------------------------------------------------------
    T2 |  .743341   .0019431   382.557  0.000      .7371573    .7495248
 _cons | -59.54193  .1690706  -352.172  0.000     -60.07999   -59.00387
-----------------------------------------------------------------------------
```

. exit, clear

Notice that the estimated coefficient on trend is the same; this is so because *T1* and *T2* have the same unit of measurement. The estimated growth rate is independent of the origin of time but when the unit of measurement is changed, care should be taken to calculate the growth over the desired period.

The estimated annual growth rate is

$$\widehat{g} = e^b - 1 = e^{0.743} - 1 = 1.102$$

To obtain the point forecast for year 1995, plug in (for this example) either $T1 = 8$ or $T2 = 95$

$$\widehat{Y}_{1995} = \exp(5.129 + .743 \times 8) = \exp(-59.542 + .743 \times 95) = 64567$$

2.2.   Denote the regressions to base e and to base 10 as

$$\ln Y = \alpha_e + \beta_e \ln X + u_e$$
$$\log Y = \alpha_{10} + \beta_{10} \log X + u_{10}$$

or in deviation form

$$y_e = \beta_e x_e + u_e$$
$$y_{10} = \beta_{10} x_{10} + u_{10}$$

Using the change of base formula, we have

$$\overline{\log X} = \sum \log X / n = \sum \ln X / (n \ln 10) = \overline{\ln X} / \ln 10$$

so

$$x_{10} = \log X - \overline{\log X} = (\ln X - \overline{\ln X}) / \ln 10 = x_e / \ln 10$$

and similary for y. The slope coefficient to base 10 is then

$$b_{10} = \frac{\sum x_{10} y_{10}}{\sum x_{10}^2} = \frac{\sum x_e y_e / (\ln 10)^2}{\sum x_e^2 / (\ln 10)^2} = \frac{\sum x_e y_e}{\sum x_e^2} = b_e$$

The slope coefficients are the same. For the intercept, we have

$$a_{10} = \overline{\log Y} - b_{10} \overline{\log X} = (\overline{\ln Y} - b_e \overline{\ln X}) / \ln 10 = a_e / \ln 10$$

so the intercepts are not the same. When the regressor is a trend, the slope coefficient to base 10 is

$$b_{10} = \frac{\sum y_{10} t}{\sum t^2} = \frac{\sum y_e t}{\ln 10 \sum t^2} = \frac{b_e}{\ln 10}$$

and the intercept is

$$a_{10} = \overline{\log Y} - b_{10}\overline{T} = (\overline{\ln Y} - b_e\overline{T})/\ln 10 = a_e/\ln 10$$

In this case both the intercept and the slope are scaled by the same factor. The general result is that when you change the unit of measurement of *both* the regressand and the regressors, the slope coefficient does not change. However, if you only change the unit of either the regressand or the regressors, the slope coefficient is also scaled.

2.3.   The log curve is concave. As an Engle curve, it may be suitable for commodities that exhibit saturation (e.g. food) but not for luxuries (diamonds?). It also has the disadvantage that expenditure becomes negative for low income.

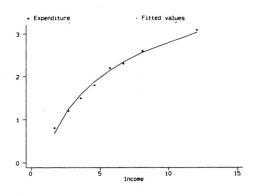

```
. reg vi lnv0

    Source |       SS       df       MS                  Number of obs =       8
-----------+------------------------------               F(  1,    6) =  607.28
     Model | 3.99923665      1  3.99923665               Prob > F      =  0.0000
  Residual | .039512903      6  .006585484               R-square      =  0.9902
-----------+------------------------------               Adj R-square  =  0.9886
     Total | 4.03874956      7  .576964223               Root MSE      =  .08115


------------------------------------------------------------------------------
        vi |      Coef.   Std. Err.       t     P>|t|     [95% Conf. Interval]
-----------+------------------------------------------------------------------
      lnv0 |   1.206553   .0489612    24.643   0.000      1.08675    1.326357
     _cons |   .0446871   .0819929     0.545   0.605     -.1559422    .2453165
------------------------------------------------------------------------------

. exit, clear
```

The income elasticity is

$$\epsilon = \frac{\nu_0}{\nu_i}\frac{\partial \nu_i}{\partial \nu_0} = \frac{\nu_0}{\nu_i}\frac{\beta}{\nu_0} = \frac{\beta}{\nu_i}$$

Therefore the point estimate of the income elasticity at $\nu_0 = 5$ is

$$\widehat{\epsilon} = \frac{b}{a + b\ln 5} = \frac{1.207}{.045 + 1.207 \times \ln 5} = .607$$

Changing the base of the log of income amounts to changing the unit of measurement of income. Since the whole point of the concept of elasticity is to make it unit free, changing the base does not affect the estimate of elasticity. To see this, let the OLS estimates to base e and to base 10 be

$$\begin{aligned} \nu_i &= a_e + b_e \ln \nu_0 \\ \nu_i &= a_{10} + b_{10} \log \nu_0 \\ &= a_{10} + b_{10} \ln \nu_0 / \ln 10 \end{aligned}$$

where the last equality follows from the change of base formula. Following the steps in Problem 2.2. we can show that

$$b_{10} = b_e \ln_e 10 \qquad \text{and} \qquad a_{10} = a_e$$

The estimated elasticity to base 10 is then

$$\widehat{\epsilon}_{10} = \frac{\nu_0}{\nu_i} \frac{\partial \nu_i}{\partial \nu_0} = \frac{\nu_0}{\nu_i} \times \frac{b_{10}}{\nu_0 \ln 10} = \frac{b_e}{\nu_i} = \widehat{\epsilon}_e$$

2.4.   The first equality follows from totally differentiating

$$d(\ln Y) = \frac{\partial \ln Y}{\partial Y} dY = \frac{dY}{Y}$$

so that

$$\frac{d(\ln Y)}{d(\ln X)} = \frac{dY}{Y} \Big/ \frac{dX}{X} = \frac{dY}{dX} \frac{X}{Y}$$

The second equality follows by using the change of base formula

$$d(\ln Y) = d(\log Y / \log e) = d(\log Y) / \log e$$

so that

$$\frac{d(\ln Y)}{d(\ln X)} = \frac{d(\log Y) / \log e}{d(\log X) / \log e} = \frac{d(\log Y)}{d(\log X)}$$

2.5.   We can rewrite the function as

$$Y = 100(1 - 1/\alpha) + \frac{100\beta}{\alpha^2 (X + \beta/\alpha)}$$

This is a hyperbola if $\alpha \neq 0$ with asymptotes $X = -\beta/\alpha$ and $Y = 100(1 - 1/\alpha)$. When $\alpha = 0$ the function is linear

$$Y = -100(X - \beta)/\beta$$

```
. gen lhs=100/(100-Y)

. gen rhs=1/X

. reg lhs rhs

  Source |       SS       df       MS                Number of obs =      10
---------+------------------------------             F( 1,    8) =  151.13
   Model | 23.6006204      1   23.6006204            Prob > F      =  0.0000
Residual | 1.24931491      8   .156164364            R-square      =  0.9497
---------+------------------------------             Adj R-square  =  0.9434
   Total | 24.8499353      9   2.76110393            Root MSE      =  .39518
```

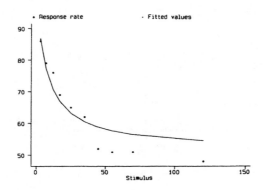

```
------------------------------------------------------------------
   lhs |    Coef.   Std. Err.      t    P>|t|    [95% Conf. Interval]
---------+--------------------------------------------------------
   rhs |  16.26623  1.323171    12.293  0.000    13.21499   19.31746
  _cons |  2.067528  .1595715    12.957  0.000    1.699555    2.4355
------------------------------------------------------------------
```

`. exit, clear`

The estimated equation is

$$\frac{100}{100 - Y} = 2.068 + \frac{16.266}{X}$$

2.6.

(a) The function

$$y = \frac{x}{\alpha x - \beta} = \frac{1}{\alpha} + \frac{\beta/\alpha^2}{x - \beta/\alpha}$$

is a hyperbola that passes through the origin (if $\alpha \neq 0$) with asymptotes $y = 1/\alpha$ and $x = \beta/\alpha$.

To make the function linear in the parameters, take the reciprocal of both sides

$$\frac{1}{y} = \frac{\alpha x - \beta}{x} = \alpha - \frac{\beta}{x}$$

(b) The logistic function

$$y = \frac{e^{\alpha + \beta x}}{1 + e^{\alpha + \beta x}} = \frac{1}{1 + e^{-\alpha - \beta x}}$$

has derivatives

$$\frac{dy}{dx} = \frac{\beta e^{-\alpha - \beta x}}{(1 + e^{-\alpha - \beta x})^2}$$

$$\frac{d^2 y}{dx^2} = \frac{\beta^2 e^{-\alpha - \beta x}(e^{-\alpha - \beta x} - 1)}{(1 + e^{-\alpha - \beta x})^3}$$

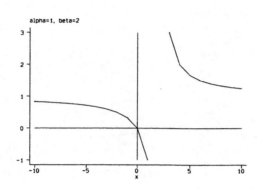

The logistic is monotone (the sign depends on the sign of β) with an inflection point at $x = -\alpha/\beta$; it asymptotes to $y = 1$ as $x \to \infty$ and to $y = 0$ as $x \to -\infty$.

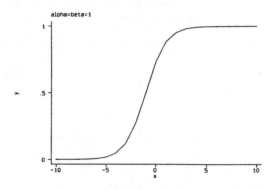

To linearize in the parameters, rewrite as

$$
\begin{aligned}
y(1 + e^{\alpha + \beta x}) &= e^{\alpha + \beta x} \\
\frac{y}{1-y} &= e^{\alpha + \beta x}
\end{aligned}
$$

and take log of both sides

$$
\ln\left(\frac{y}{1-y}\right) = \alpha + \beta x
$$

2.7.

```
. reg Y T
```

```
  Source |       SS       df       MS                Number of obs =      18
---------+------------------------------             F(  1,    16) =  277.44
   Model | 7783.14706      1  7783.14706             Prob > F      =  0.0000
Residual | 448.852941     16  28.0533088             R-square      =  0.9455
---------+------------------------------             Adj R-square  =  0.9421
   Total |    8232.00     17  484.235294             Root MSE      =  5.2965


-------------------------------------------------------------------------------
       Y |    Coef.   Std. Err.       t     P>|t|     [95% Conf. Interval]
---------+---------------------------------------------------------------------
       T | 17.47059   1.048871    16.657    0.000     15.24708    19.69409
   _cons | 99.05882   2.441114    40.579    0.000     93.88389    104.2338
-------------------------------------------------------------------------------

. reg AVG T

  Source |       SS       df       MS                Number of obs =       6
---------+------------------------------             F(  1,     4) =  465.69
   Model | 2594.38182      1  2594.38182             Prob > F      =  0.0000
Residual |  22.284323      4  5.57108075             R-square      =  0.9915
---------+------------------------------             Adj R-square  =  0.9894
   Total | 2616.66614      5  523.333229             Root MSE      =  2.3603


-------------------------------------------------------------------------------
     AVG |    Coef.   Std. Err.       t     P>|t|     [95% Conf. Interval]
---------+---------------------------------------------------------------------
       T | 17.47059   .8095809    21.580    0.000     15.22283    19.71834
   _cons | 99.05883   1.884197    52.573    0.000     93.82746    104.2902
-------------------------------------------------------------------------------
```

Notice that the two regressions have almost identical coefficients. But the second regression of the conditional means has a tighter fit (larger R^2 and smaller standard errors). When data are available only in group averages, care should be taken in interpreting the regression results.

2.8.

$$Y = a + b\left(\frac{1}{1-X}\right)$$

is a hyperbola with asymptotes $X = 1$ and $Y = a$.

```
. gen rhs = 1/(1-X)

. reg Y rhs

  Source |       SS       df       MS                Number of obs =       3
---------+------------------------------             F(  1,     1) =  133.33
   Model | 20.5128203      1  20.5128203             Prob > F      =  0.0550
Residual |  .15384638      1   .15384638             R-square      =  0.9926
---------+------------------------------             Adj R-square  =  0.9851
   Total | 20.6666667      2  10.3333333             Root MSE      =  .39223


-------------------------------------------------------------------------------
       Y |    Coef.   Std. Err.       t     P>|t|     [95% Conf. Interval]
---------+---------------------------------------------------------------------
     rhs | 1.538462   .1332348    11.547    0.055     -.1544468   3.231371
   _cons | 7.769231   .4213254    18.440    0.034     2.415785   13.12268
-------------------------------------------------------------------------------
```

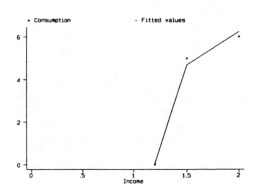

The estimated equation is

$$Y = 7.769 + \frac{1.538}{1 - X}$$

Since $Y \to a$ as $X \to \infty$, peanut consumption of a millionaire will be about 7.7.

2.9.

```
. gen rhs = 1/X

. reg Y rhs
```

Source	SS	df	MS		Number of obs =	4
					F(1, 2) =	36287.98
Model	265.98534	1	265.98534		Prob > F =	0.0000
Residual	.014659695	2	.007329848		R-square =	0.9999
					Adj R-square =	0.9999
Total	266.00	3	88.6666667		Root MSE =	.08561

Y	Coef.	Std. Err.	t	P>|t|	[95% Conf. Interval]	
rhs	21.10995	.1108168	190.494	0.000	20.63314	21.58675
_cons	9.875393	.0568443	173.727	0.000	9.630811	10.11997

The estimated equation is

$$Y = 9.875 + \frac{21.110}{X}$$

The estimated minimum cost is the asymptote $Y = a = 9.875$. To get the estimate of the batch size that brings average cost within 10 percent of the minimum, solve

$$1.1a = a + \frac{b}{X}$$

to get

$$X = \frac{10b}{a} = \frac{10 \times 21.110}{9.875} = 21.377$$

23

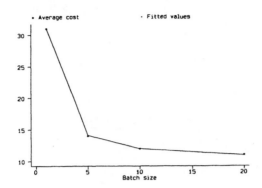

2.10. This is a well known (pathological) example where the plim is *not* the limit of the mean. Consider first the plim of x_n. Looking at the density function, we find that as $n \to \infty$, $x_n = 1$ with probability 1. Therefore $\text{plim}\, x_n = 1$. More formally, for any positive ϵ and δ

$$\Pr(|\, x_n - 1 \,|> \epsilon) = \Pr(x_n = n) = \frac{1}{n} < \delta \qquad \text{for any } n > \frac{1}{\delta}.$$

The mean and variance of x_n are

$$E(x_n) = 1 - \frac{1}{n} + n \times \frac{1}{n} = 2 - \frac{1}{n} \to 2 \quad \text{as } n \to \infty$$

$$\begin{aligned}
var(x_n) &= E(x_n^2) - [E(x_n)]^2 \\
&= 1 - \frac{1}{n} + n^2 \times \frac{1}{n} - \left(2 - \frac{1}{n}\right)^2 \\
&= n - 1 + \frac{3}{n} - \frac{1}{n^2} \to \infty \quad \text{as } n \to \infty
\end{aligned}$$

Notice two things. First, the limit of the mean is not equal to the plim. Second, the plim can exist even when the variance does not converge to zero.

2.11. In each case write down the likelihood function, take logs, and solve the first order conditions.

(a) Bernoulli distribution

$$\begin{aligned}
L(\theta; x) &= f(x_1)f(x_2)\cdots f(x_n) \\
&= \theta^{x_1}(1-\theta)^{1-x_1}\theta^{x_2}(1-\theta)^{1-x_2}\cdots\theta^{x_n}(1-\theta)^{1-x_n} \\
&= \theta^{\sum x}(1-\theta)^{n-\sum x} \\
\ell &= \ln L \\
&= \sum x \ln\theta + (n - \sum x)\ln(1-\theta)
\end{aligned}$$

The first order condition is

$$\frac{\partial \ell}{\partial \theta} = \frac{\sum x}{\theta} - \frac{n - \sum x}{1 - \theta} = 0$$

which gives the MLE

$$\hat{\theta} = \frac{\sum x}{n} = \bar{x}$$

This is just the sample mean. The second derivative is

$$\frac{\partial^2 \ell}{\partial \theta^2} = -\frac{\sum x}{\theta^2} - \frac{n - \sum x}{(1 - \theta)^2} < 0$$

since $x = 0, 1$ and $0 \le \sum x \le n$.

(b) Poisson distribution

$$
\begin{aligned}
L(\theta; x) &= f(x_1)f(x_2)\cdots f(x_n) \\
&= \frac{\theta^{x_1} e^{-\theta}}{x_1!} \frac{\theta^{x_2} e^{-\theta}}{x_2!} \cdots \frac{\theta^{x_n} e^{-\theta}}{x_n!} \\
&= \frac{\theta^{\sum x} e^{-n\theta}}{x_1! x_2! \cdots x_n!} \\
\ell &= \ln L \\
&= \sum x \ln \theta - n\theta - \ln(x_1! x_2! \cdots x_n!)
\end{aligned}
$$

The first order condition is

$$\frac{\partial \ell}{\partial \theta} = \frac{\sum x}{\theta} - n = 0$$

which gives the MLE

$$\hat{\theta} = \frac{\sum x}{n} = \bar{x}$$

Again this is the sample mean. The second derivative is

$$\frac{\partial^2 \ell}{\partial \theta^2} = -\frac{\sum x}{\theta^2} < 0$$

since $x \ge 0$.

(c) Exponential distribution

$$
\begin{aligned}
L(\theta; x) &= f(x_1)f(x_2)\cdots f(x_n) \\
&= \theta e^{-\theta x_1} \theta e^{-\theta x_2} \cdots \theta e^{-\theta x_n} \\
&= \theta^n e^{-\theta \sum x} \\
\ell &= \ln L \\
&= n \ln \theta - \theta \sum x
\end{aligned}
$$

The first order condition is

$$\frac{\partial \ell}{\partial \theta} = \frac{n}{\theta} - \sum x = 0$$

which gives the MLE

$$\widehat{\theta} = \frac{n}{\sum x} = \frac{1}{\overline{x}}$$

This is the reciprocal of the sample mean. The second derivative is

$$\frac{\partial^2 \ell}{\partial \theta^2} = -\frac{n}{\theta^2} < 0$$

2.12. I generated two independent standard normal variables $u_{1,t}$ and $u_{2,t}$ and generated six series (all with initial value zero)

$$
\begin{aligned}
x_{j,t} &= 0.9x_{j,t-1} + u_{j,t} \\
y_{j,t} &= y_{j,t-1} + u_{j,t} \\
z_{j,t} &= 1.05z_{j,t-1} + u_{j,t}
\end{aligned}
$$

for $j = 1, 2$. x_j are two independent stationary series, y_j are two independent random walks, and z_j are two independent explosive series. The correlations of successive 50 observations are

Sample	$corr(x_1, x_2)$	$corr(y_1, y_2)$	$corr(z_1, z_2)$
51–100	.4654	.5508	−.9997
101–150	.8280	.7804	−1.000
151–200	−.5021	−.7360	−1.000
201–250	.5592	.5083	−1.000
251–300	−.0238	.4072	−1.000
301–350	−.1393	.2185	−1.000
351–400	.4989	.5258	−1.000
401–450	.0306	−.4331	−1.000
451–500	−.1458	.7527	−1.000
501–550	−.0598	−.3708	−1.000
551–600	.2953	−.2693	−1.000
601–650	−.4097	.1270	−1.000
651–700	−.4302	−.8807	−1.000
701–750	−.0826	−.8769	−1.000
751–800	−.0049	.0133	−1.000
801–850	−.1984	.6342	−1.000
851–900	−.0789	−.0667	−1.000
901–950	.2838	−.6099	−1.000
951–1000	−.3088	−.8170	−1.000

Note that the correlations between two independent non-stationary series (y and z) are generally larger than those between the stationary series (x), especially near the end of the sample.

Chapter 3

3.1. The normal equations in raw data are $X'Xb = X'y$. If we partition X as $X = [i \; X_{-1}]$, the normal equations can be written as

$$\begin{bmatrix} n & i'X_{-1} \\ X'_{-1}i & X'_{-1}X_{-1} \end{bmatrix} \begin{bmatrix} b_1 \\ b_{-1} \end{bmatrix} = \begin{bmatrix} i'y \\ X'_{-1}y \end{bmatrix}$$

Apply the Gaussian elimination as follows. Pre-multiply the first row by $X'_{-1}i/n$ and subtract from the remaining $(k-1)$ rows. The result is

$$\begin{bmatrix} n & i'X_{-1} \\ 0 & X'_{-1}X_{-1} - X'_{-1}ii'X_{-1}/n \end{bmatrix} \begin{bmatrix} b_1 \\ b_{-1} \end{bmatrix} = \begin{bmatrix} i'y \\ X'_{-1}y - X'_{-1}ii'y/n \end{bmatrix}$$

The last $(k-1)$ equations can be written as

$$X'_{-1}AX_{-1}b_{-1} = X'_{-1}Ay$$

where $A = I - ii'/n$ is the deviation-from-means operator. These are the normal equations in deviation form.

3.2. Follow the same steps as in Appendix 3.1. We start from

$$r_{13.2} = \frac{\sum e_{1.2}e_{3.2}}{\sqrt{\sum e_{1.2}^2}\sqrt{\sum e_{3.2}^2}}$$

where

$$e_{1.2} = y - b_{12}x_2 = y - r_{12}\frac{s_1}{s_2}x_2$$

$$e_{3.2} = x_3 - b_{32}x_2 = x_3 - r_{23}\frac{s_3}{s_2}x_2$$

are the residuals from regressing y and x_3 on x_2. We want to express all the terms on the right-hand side of $r_{13.2}$ in terms of simple correlations. We have

$$\sum e_{1.2}^2 = \sum y^2(1 - r_{12}^2) = (1 - r_{12}^2)ns_1^2$$

$$\sum e_{3.2}^2 = \sum x_3^2(1 - r_{23}^2) = (1 - r_{23}^2)ns_3^2$$

and

$$\begin{aligned} \sum e_{1.2}e_{3.2} &= \sum \left(y - r_{12}\frac{s_1}{s_2}x_2\right)\left(x_3 - r_{23}\frac{s_3}{s_2}x_2\right) \\ &= \sum yx_3 - r_{23}\frac{s_3}{s_2}\sum yx_2 - r_{12}\frac{s_1}{s_2}\sum x_2x_3 + r_{12}r_{23}\frac{s_1s_3}{s_2^2}\sum x_2^2 \end{aligned}$$

27

Substitute the definition of the correlation coefficient $\sum xy = ns_x s_y r_{xy}$ to get

$$
\begin{aligned}
\sum e_{1.2} e_{3.2} &= ns_1 s_3 r_{13} - r_{23}\frac{s_3}{s_2}ns_1 s_2 r_{12} - r_{12}\frac{s_1}{s_2}ns_2 s_3 r_{23} + r_{12}r_{23}\frac{s_1 s_3}{s_2^2}ns_2^2 \\
&= ns_1 s_3 (r_{13} - r_{12}r_{23})
\end{aligned}
$$

Putting the results together we have

$$
r_{13.2} = \frac{ns_1 s_3 (r_{13} - r_{12}r_{23})}{\sqrt{ns_1^2(1 - r_{12}^2)}\sqrt{ns_3^2(1 - r_{23}^2)}} = \frac{r_{13} - r_{12}r_{23}}{\sqrt{1 - r_{12}^2}\sqrt{1 - r_{23}^2}}
$$

3.3.

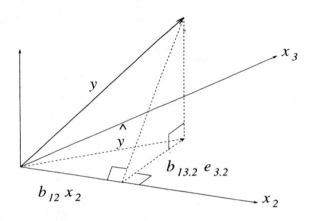

First decompose $\hat{y}$, the projection of y on x_2 and x_3, as $\hat{y} = b_{12}x_2 + b_{13.2}e_{3.2}$. This can be most easily understood geometrically. First, project y onto x_2. This is the first term $b_{12}x_2$. We next project the residual $e_{1.2}$ from this projection on $e_{3.2}$, the residual from projecting x_3 on x_2. This is the second term $b_{13.2}e_{3.2}$. Notice that $e_{3.2}$ is orthogonal to x_2. Therefore we have an orthogonal decomposition of $\hat{y}$. The ESS is then

$$
\hat{y}'\hat{y} = b_{12}^2 x_2' x_2 + b_{13.2}^2 e_{3.2}' e_{3.2}
$$

The first term can be written as

$$
b_{12}^2 x_2' x_2 = r_{12}^2 (y'y/x_2'x_2)x_2'x_2 = r_{12}^2 y'y
$$

while the second term is

$$
b_{13.2}^2 e_{3.2}' e_{3.2} = r_{13.2}^2 (e_{1.2}'e_{1.2}/e_{3.2}'e_{3.2})e_{3.2}'e_{3.2} = r_{13.2}^2 (1 - r_{12}^2)y'y
$$

Therefore

$$
ESS = \left(r_{12}^2 + r_{13.2}^2(1 - r_{12}^2)\right)y'y
$$

and

$$
R^2 = \frac{ESS}{TSS} = r_{12}^2 + r_{13.2}^2(1 - r_{12}^2)
$$

The other formula can be shown similarly; first project y on x_3 and then project the residual on $e_{2.3}$. This gives the orthogonal decomposition $\hat{y} = b_{13}x_3 + b_{12.3}e_{2.3}$.

To show the corollary, when $r_{23} = 0$ the partial correlation is

$$r_{13.2} = \frac{r_{13} - r_{12}r_{23}}{\sqrt{1 - r_{12}^2}\sqrt{1 - r_{23}^2}} = \frac{r_{13}}{\sqrt{1 - r_{12}^2}}$$

Substituting in the first formula gives $R^2 = r_{12}^2 + r_{13}^2$. In this case the orthogonal decomposition is $\hat{y} = b_{12}x_2 + b_{13}x_3$.

3.4.   The normal equations are

$$\begin{bmatrix} p'p & p't \\ t'p & t't \end{bmatrix} \begin{bmatrix} b_2 \\ b_3 \end{bmatrix} = \begin{bmatrix} p'q \\ t'q \end{bmatrix}$$

$$\begin{bmatrix} b_2 \\ b_3 \end{bmatrix} = \frac{1}{(p'p)(t't) - (p't)^2} \begin{bmatrix} t't & -p't \\ -t'p & p'p \end{bmatrix} \begin{bmatrix} p'q \\ t'q \end{bmatrix}$$

and

$$\begin{aligned}
b_3 &= \frac{(p'p)(t'q) - (p'q)(t'p)}{(p'p)(t't) - (p't)^2} \\
&= \frac{t'q/t't - (p'q/p'p)(t'p/t't)}{1 - (p't/t't)(p't/p'p)} \\
&= \frac{b_{13} - b_{12}b_{23}}{1 - b_{23}b_{32}}
\end{aligned}$$

Alternatively, from the OLS formula

$$\begin{aligned}
b_{13.2} &= \frac{e'_{1.2}e_{3.2}}{e'_{3.2}e_{3.2}} \\
&= \frac{(q - b_{12}p)'(t - b_{32}p)}{(t - b_{32}p)'(t - b_{32}p)} \\
&= \frac{q't - b_{32}q'p - b_{12}p't + b_{12}b_{32}p'p}{t't - 2b_{32}t'p + b_{32}^2 p'p} \\
&= \frac{b_{13}t't - b_{32}b_{12}p'p - b_{12}b_{23}t't + b_{12}b_{32}p'p}{t't - 2b_{32}b_{23}t't + b_{32}b_{23}t't} \\
&= \frac{b_{13} - b_{12}b_{23}}{1 - b_{23}b_{32}} \\
&= b_3
\end{aligned}$$

When $b_{23} = 0$, the two regressors are orthogonal. In this case $b_3 = b_{13.2} = b_{13}$ and $b_2 = b_{12.3} = b_{12}$.

3.5. $M = I - X(X'X)^{-1}X'$ is the residual maker matrix; My gives the residuals from regressing y on X. The residuals from regressing y on a constant $X = i$ is then

$$My = \left(I - i(i'i)^{-1}i'\right)y = (I - ii'/n)y = Ay = y_*$$

and $y'_* y_*$ is the RSS. The estimated coefficient is

$$b = (X'X)^{-1}X'y = (i'i)^{-1}i'y = \sum y/n = \overline{Y}$$

3.6.   The regression can be written as

$$y = ib_1 + X_* b_2 + e$$

Pre-multiply both sides by the deviation-from-means matrix $A = I - ii'/n$ to get

$$y_* = X_* b_2 + e$$

From the OLS formula we have

$$b_2 = (X'_* X_*)^{-1} X'_* y_* = (X'_* X_*)^{-1} X'_* A y = (X'_* X_*)^{-1} X'_* y$$

To get b_1, recall that the regression plane passes through the mean. But the mean of X_* is a null vector, so $b_1 = \overline{Y}$.

The estimmated variance of the (conditional) forecast is

$$
\begin{aligned}
var(\widehat{Y}_f) &= E[E(Y) - \widehat{Y}]^2 \\
&= E(x'\beta - x'b)^2 \\
&= x' E(\beta - b)(\beta - b)' x \\
&= s^2 x' (X'X)^{-1} x \\
&= s^2 [1\ x'_*] \left(\begin{bmatrix} i' \\ X'_* \end{bmatrix} [i\ X_*] \right)^{-1} \begin{bmatrix} 1 \\ x_* \end{bmatrix} \\
&= s^2 [1\ x'_*] \begin{bmatrix} 1/n & 0 \\ 0 & (X'_* X_*)^{-1} \end{bmatrix} \begin{bmatrix} 1 \\ x_* \end{bmatrix} \\
&= s^2 \left[\frac{1}{n} + x'_* (X'_* X_*)^{-1} x_* \right]
\end{aligned}
$$

In Example 3.8

$$x'_* (X'_* X_*)^{-1} x_* = [7\ 5] \begin{bmatrix} 10 & 6 \\ 6 & 4 \end{bmatrix}^{-1} \begin{bmatrix} 7 \\ 5 \end{bmatrix} = 6.5$$

and so the 95% confidence interval of $E(Y_f)$ can be obtained as

$$
\begin{aligned}
& \widehat{Y} \pm t_{.975}(2) \sqrt{ s^2 \left(\frac{1}{n} + x'_* (X'_* X_*)^{-1} x_* \right) } \\
&= 14 \pm 4.303 \sqrt{ 0.75 \left(\frac{1}{5} + 6.5 \right) } \\
&= 4.35 \quad \text{to} \quad 23.65
\end{aligned}
$$

3.7.

(a) The R^2 cannot decrease by adding variables. If the added variable does not help explain the regressand at all, the estimated coefficient will simply be zero and the part explained by the regressors will be the same. Note that for this result to hold, you have to retain all the previous variables. For instance, nothing can be said about $R^2_{1.23}$ and $R^2_{1.245}$.

(b) We use Eq. (3.16)

$$R^2_{1.23} = r^2_{12} + r^2_{13.2}(1 - r^2_{12}) = r^2_{13} + r^2_{12.3}(1 - r^2_{13})$$

to check whether $r_{13.2}^2$ and $r_{12.3}^2$ lie between 0 and 1:

$$r_{13.2}^2 = \frac{R^2 - r_{12}^2}{1 - r_{12}^2} = .613$$

$$r_{12.3}^2 = \frac{R^2 - r_{13}^2}{1 - r_{13}^2} = .658$$

so the given results seem to be possible. As a further check, we can also calculate r_{23} to see if it has absolute value less than 1. Solving Eq. (3.15)

$$r_{13.2} = \frac{r_{13} - r_{12}r_{23}}{\sqrt{1 - r_{12}^2}\sqrt{1 - r_{23}^2}}$$

for r_{23} yields a quadratic

$$\left(r_{12}^2 + r_{13.2}^2(1 - r_{12}^2)\right) r_{23}^2 - 2r_{12}r_{13}r_{23} + r_{13}^2 - r_{13.2}^2(1 - r_{12}^2) = 0$$
$$R^2 r_{23}^2 - 2r_{12}r_{13}r_{23} + r_{12}^2 + r_{13}^2 - R^2 = 0$$

Let $f(x) = R^2 x^2 - 2r_{12}r_{13}x + r_{12}^2 + r_{13}^2 - R^2$. Then

$$f(\pm 1) = (r_{12} \mp r_{13})^2 > 0$$

$$f(0) = r_{12}^2 + r_{13}^2 - R^2 = -0.348 < 0$$

so the two roots of r_{23} lie between -1 and 1.

(c) From the Cauchy-Schwarz inequality,

$$r^2 = \frac{\left(\sum xy\right)^2}{\sum x^2 \sum y^2} \leq 1$$

Therefore

$$\left(\sum x^2\right)\left(\sum y^2\right) - \left(\sum xy\right)^2 \geq 0$$

and the given result is impossible.

3.8. Multiply both sides of the standardized regression by s_y to get

$$Y = s_y\beta_1^* + \frac{s_y}{s_2}\beta_2^* X_2 + \frac{s_y}{s_3}\beta_3^* X_3$$

This is the original regression. Comparing the coefficients, we have

$$\beta_1^* = \frac{1}{s_y}\beta_1, \qquad \beta_2^* = \frac{s_2}{s_y}\beta_2, \qquad \beta_3^* = \frac{s_3}{s_y}\beta_3$$

From Eqs. (3.14) and (3.15) the partial correlation coefficients can be expressed in terms of simple correlations. Problem 1.12 shows that the simple correlations are invariant to linear transformations so the partial correlation coefficients are also invariant to linear transformations.

3.9.   The estimated slope coefficients are

$$b = \begin{bmatrix} 10 & 10 & 5 \\ 10 & 30 & 15 \\ 5 & 15 & 20 \end{bmatrix}^{-1} \begin{bmatrix} 7 \\ -7 \\ -26 \end{bmatrix} = \begin{bmatrix} 1.4 \\ 0.2 \\ -1.8 \end{bmatrix}$$

and

$$s^2 = \frac{e'e}{n-k} = \frac{y'y - b'X'y}{n-k} = \frac{60 - 55.2}{20} = 0.24$$

The estimated covariance matrix is

$$E(b-\beta)(b-\beta)' = s^2(X'X)^{-1} = 0.24 \begin{bmatrix} 0.15 & -0.05 & 0 \\ -0.05 & 0.07 & -0.04 \\ 0 & -0.04 & 0.08 \end{bmatrix}$$

The test statistics for each hypotheses $\beta_1 = 1$, $\beta_2 = 1$, $\beta_3 = -2$ are

$$t_1 = \frac{b_1 - 1}{s.e.(b_1)} = \frac{1.4 - 1}{\sqrt{0.036}} = 2.108$$

$$t_2 = \frac{b_2 - 1}{s.e.(b_2)} = \frac{0.2 - 1}{\sqrt{0.0168}} = -6.172$$

$$t_3 = \frac{b_3 - (-2)}{s.e.(b_3)} = \frac{-1.8 + 2}{\sqrt{0.0192}} = 1.4434$$

The 5% critical value is $t_{.975}(20) = 2.086$. We therefore reject (at 5% significance level) the first two hypotheses $\beta_1 = 1$, $\beta_2 = 1$ but not the third $\beta_3 = -2$.

To calculate the test statistic for the hypothesis $\beta_1 + \beta_2 + \beta_3 = 0$ I use Eq. (3.39). In this case $R = [1\ 1\ 1]$ and $r = 0$ and the term $s^2 R(X'X)^{-1} R'$ is the sum of all elements of the covariance matrix. Then

$$F = \frac{(b_1 + b_2 + b_3)^2/q}{s^2 R(X'X)^{-1}R'} = \frac{0.04}{0.24 \times 0.12} = 1.389$$

The 5% critical value is $F_{.950}(1, 20) = 4.35$ and we cannot reject (at 5% significance level) the hypothesis that the slope coefficients sum to zero.

The hypothesis $[\beta_1\ \beta_2\ \beta_3] = [1\ 1\ -2]$ is a special case of the previous hypothesis. Since it imposes a stronger restriction we expect the test statistic to be larger. In this case R is the identity matrix and $r' = [1\ 1\ -2]$. The test statistic is

$$F = \frac{(b-r)'X'X(b-r)/q}{s^2} = \frac{11.2/3}{0.24} = 15.556$$

The 5% critical value is $F_{.95}(3, 20) = 3.10$ and we reject (at 5% significance level) this stronger hypothesis.

3.10.   One way is to invert the 3×3 matrix including the constant. However, it is easier to work in deviation form. The data in deviation form are

$$\sum y^2 = \sum Y^2 - (\sum Y)^2/n = 48.2$$

$$\sum x_1^2 = \sum X_1^2 - (\sum X_1)^2/n = 2$$

$$\sum x_2^2 = \sum X_2^2 - (\sum X_2)^2/n = 3$$

$$\sum x_1 x_2 = \sum X_1 X_2 - \sum X_1 \sum X_2/n = -1$$

$$\sum y x_1 = \sum Y X_1 - \sum Y \sum X_1/n = -1$$

$$\sum y x_2 = \sum Y X_2 - \sum Y \sum X_2/n = 8$$

The OLS slope estimates are

$$b = \begin{bmatrix} 2 & -1 \\ -1 & 3 \end{bmatrix}^{-1} \begin{bmatrix} -1 \\ 8 \end{bmatrix} = \begin{bmatrix} 1 \\ 3 \end{bmatrix}$$

and the intercept is

$$b_0 = \overline{Y} - b_1 \overline{X}_1 - b_2 \overline{X}_2 = -7$$

The estimated equation is

$$Y = -7 + X_1 + 3X_2$$

The estimated residual variance is

$$s^2 = \frac{e'e}{n-k} = \frac{y'y - b'X'y}{n-k} = \frac{48.2 - 23}{7} = 3.6$$

and the estimated covariance matrix is

$$E(b - \beta)(b - \beta)' = s^2(X'X)^{-1} = 3.6 \begin{bmatrix} 0.6 & 0.2 \\ 0.2 & 0.4 \end{bmatrix} = \begin{bmatrix} 2.16 & 0.72 \\ 0.72 & 1.44 \end{bmatrix}$$

The test statistic for the hypothesis $\beta_2 = 0$ is

$$t = \frac{b_2}{s.e.(b_2)} = \frac{3}{\sqrt{1.44}} = 2.5$$

The critical values are $t_{.975}(7) = 2.365$ and $t_{.995}(7) = 3.500$. We reject $\beta_2 = 0$ at 5% significance level but not at 1% significance level.

3.11. We do not have an estimate of the residual variance s^2 itself, but we have an estimate of the covariance matrix $s^2(X'X)^{-1}$. This enables us to carry out the F-test. But since each hypothesis consists of a single restriction, I carry out the simpler t-test instead.

(a) The hypothesis is $\beta_k - \beta_l = 0$ with test statistic

$$\begin{aligned} t &= \frac{b_k - b_l}{\sqrt{\text{var}(b_k - b_l)}} \\ &= \frac{b_k - b_l}{\sqrt{\text{var}(b_k) - 2\text{cov}(b_k, b_l) + \text{var}(b_l)}} \\ &= \frac{0.632 - 0.452}{\sqrt{0.257^2 - 2 \times 0.055 + 0.219^2}} \\ &= 2.846 \end{aligned}$$

In order to get the critical values we need the sample size. Looking at the t-table we find that if $n - k > 3$ or $n > 6$, we reject the hypothesis at 5% significance level.

(*b*) The hypothesis is $\beta_k + \beta_l = 1$ with test statistic

$$
\begin{aligned}
t &= \frac{b_k + b_l - 1}{\sqrt{\mathrm{var}(b_k + b_l)}} \\
&= \frac{b_k + b_l - 1}{\sqrt{\mathrm{var}(b_k) + 2\mathrm{cov}(b_k, b_l) + \mathrm{var}(b_l)}} \\
&= \frac{0.632 + 0.452 - 1}{\sqrt{0.257^2 + 2 \times 0.055 + 0.219^2}} \\
&= 0.178
\end{aligned}
$$

This is not significant for any sample size. We cannot reject the hypothesis of constant returns to scale.

3.12.   It is easiest to contrast the residual sum of squares from the restricted (RSS_*) and unrestricted (RSS) regressions. In this case the restricted regression does not have any regressors, so $ESS_* = 0$ and $RSS_* = TSS$. The test statistic is then

$$
F = \frac{(RSS_* - RSS)/q}{RSS/(n - k + 1)} = \frac{(TSS - RSS)/(k - 1)}{RSS/(n - k + 1)} = \frac{ESS/(k - 1)}{RSS/(n - k + 1)}
$$

This is distributed as $F(k - 1, n - k + 1)$ under the null hypothesis.

3.13.   Under rational expecations, the regression

$$
r = \alpha + \beta r^* + u
$$

should yield $a = 0$ *and* $b = 1$. We can carry out this joint test by the F-test in Eq. (3.38). In this case R is the identity matrix and $r' = [0\ 1]$. The test statistic is

$$
\begin{aligned}
F &= \frac{(Rb - r)'[R(X'X)^{-1}R']^{-1}(Rb - r)/q}{e'e/(n - k)} \\
&= \frac{(b - r)'X'X(b - r)/q}{e'e/(n - k)} \\
&= \frac{[0.24\ -0.06] \begin{bmatrix} 30 & 300 \\ 300 & 3052 \end{bmatrix} \begin{bmatrix} 0.24 \\ -0.06 \end{bmatrix} /2}{28.56/28} \\
&= 1.998
\end{aligned}
$$

The 5% critical value is $F_{.950}(2, 28) = 3.34$. The test statistic is not significant and we cannot reject the rational expectations hypothesis (at 5% significance level).

3.14.

(*a*) In this data x_1 and x_2 are orthogonal ($\sum x_1 x_2 = 0$). Then each coefficient is the same as that from the simple regression. Thus

$$
b_1 = \frac{\sum x_1 y}{\sum x_1^2} = 1
$$

$$
b_2 = \frac{\sum x_2 y}{\sum x_2^2} = \frac{20}{3} = 6.667
$$

From the orthogonality condition, the *ESS* is

$$\hat{y}'\hat{y} = b_1 x_1' y + b_2 x_2' y = 30 + \frac{20}{3} \times 20 = \frac{490}{3}$$

and

$$R^2 = \frac{\hat{y}'\hat{y}}{y'y} = \frac{490/3}{493/3} = .994$$

(b) To make inferences, we need an estimate of the residual variance s^2.

$$RSS = TSS - ESS = \frac{493}{3} - \frac{490}{3} = 1$$

so

$$s^2 = \frac{RSS}{n-k} = \frac{1}{97}$$

The estimated covariance matrix is

$$var(b) = s^2(X'X)^{-1} = \begin{bmatrix} 3.436 & 0 \\ 0 & 34.364 \end{bmatrix} \times 10^{-4}$$

The test statistic for the hypothesis $\beta_2 = 7$ is

$$t = \frac{b_2 - 7}{s.e.(b_2)} = \frac{6.667 - 7}{\sqrt{34.364 \times 10^{-4}}} = -5.686$$

This is significant at conventional significance levels and we reject the hypothesis.

(c) This is the test for the joint significance of the slope coefficients. The F-statistic in Eq. (3.40) is

$$F = \frac{ESS/(k-1)}{RSS/(n-k)} = \frac{(490/3)/2}{1/97} = 7921.7$$

This is highly significant and we reject the hypothesis.

(d) In this case $R = [7 \ -1]$ and $r = 0$. The test statistic in Eq. (3.38) is then

$$F = \frac{(Rb)'[R(X'X)^{-1}R']^{-1}Rb/q}{e'e/(n-k)} = \frac{(1/3)^2(59/30)^{-1}}{1/97} = 5.480$$

The 5% critical value is $F_{.950}(1, 100) = 3.94$ and we again reject the hypothesis.

3.15.   Working in deviation form, the four regressions tell us that

$$\frac{\sum c_t y_t}{\sum y_t^2} = .92, \quad \frac{\sum c_t c_{t-1}}{\sum c_{t-1}^2} = .84, \quad \frac{\sum c_{t-1} y_t}{\sum y_t^2} = .78, \quad \frac{\sum y_t c_{t-1}}{\sum c_{t-1}^2} = .55$$

These are five summations (unknowns) in four equations. My strategy is to write all summations in terms of, say, $\sum y_t c_{t-1}$. Then

$$\sum y_t^2 = \frac{1}{.78} \sum y_t c_{t-1}$$

$$\sum c_{t-1}^2 = \frac{1}{.55} \sum y_t c_{t-1}$$

$$\sum c_t y_t = .92 \quad \sum y_t^2 = \frac{92}{78} \quad \sum y_t c_{t-1}$$

$$\sum c_t c_{t-1} = .84 \quad \sum c_{t-1}^2 = \frac{84}{55} \quad \sum y_t c_{t-1}$$

The normal equations for the regression in deviation form

$$c_t = \beta_2 y_t + \beta_3 c_{t-1} + u_t$$

give

$$
\begin{aligned}
b &= \begin{bmatrix} \sum y_t^2 & \sum y_t c_{t-1} \\ \sum c_{t-1} y_t & \sum c_{t-1}^2 \end{bmatrix}^{-1} \begin{bmatrix} \sum y_t c_t \\ \sum c_{t-1} c_t \end{bmatrix} \\
&= \begin{bmatrix} 1/.78 & 1 \\ 1 & 1/.55 \end{bmatrix}^{-1} \begin{bmatrix} 92/78 \\ 84/55 \end{bmatrix} \\
&= \begin{bmatrix} 0.464 \\ 0.585 \end{bmatrix}
\end{aligned}
$$

3.16.   We have the orthogonal decomposition

$$y = Xb + e = \widehat{y} + e$$

Pre-multiplying both sides by the deviation-from-mean matrix $A = I - ii'/n$ yields

$$Ay = A\widehat{y} + e$$

Further pre-multiply both sides by the transpose of $\widehat{y}$ and notice that the last term vanishes from the orthogonality condition.

$$\widehat{y}'Ay = \widehat{y}A\widehat{y}$$

or

$$\sum (\widehat{y} - \overline{\overline{y}})(y - \overline{y}) = \sum (\widehat{y} - \overline{\overline{y}})^2$$

Therefore

$$r^2_{y\widehat{y}} = \frac{\left(\sum (\widehat{y} - \overline{\overline{y}})(y - \overline{y}) \right)^2}{\sum (y - \overline{y})^2 \sum (\widehat{y} - \overline{\overline{y}})^2} = \frac{\sum (\widehat{y} - \overline{\overline{y}})^2}{\sum (y - \overline{y})^2} = R^2$$

3.17.   The residual sum is

$$i'e = i'(y - \widehat{y}) = i'(y - Py) = i'(I - P)y = i'My$$

where $P = X(X'X)^{-1}X'$ is the projection matrix and $M = I - P$ is the residual maker matrix. The term $i'M$ is the residual from regressing the constant i on X. If X includes a constant, then the fit will be perfect with zero residual ($i'M = 0$). But if X does not include a constant the residual $i'M$ will not be zero in general.

Consider the orthogonal decomposition in deviation form

$$Ay = A\widehat{y} + Ae$$

Note that $Ae = e$ no longer holds when e does not sum to zero. Squaring both sides gives

$$
\begin{aligned}
y'Ay &= \widehat{y}'A\widehat{y} + 2\widehat{y}Ae + e'Ae \\
&= \widehat{y}'A\widehat{y} + 2\widehat{y}Ae + e'e - e'Pe \\
y'Ay - e'e &= \widehat{y}'A\widehat{y} + 2\widehat{y}Ae - e'Pe
\end{aligned}
$$

where $P = ii'/n$ is now a projection on the constant i. The R^2 is

$$R^2 = 1 - \frac{e'e}{y'Ay} = \frac{y'Ay - e'e}{y'Ay} = \frac{\hat{y}'A\hat{y} + 2\hat{y}Ae - e'Pe}{y'Ay}$$

When e has zero mean, the last two terms in the numerator are zero and R^2 is non-negative. But otherwise, the numerator can be negative.

3.18.   We first prove that $\overline{R}^2$ increases when the F statistic of the added variable exceeds 1. From Eq. (3.11)

$$\overline{R}_k^2 = 1 - \frac{e_k'e_k/(n-k)}{y'y/(n-1)}$$

$$\overline{R}_{k+1}^2 = 1 - \frac{e_{k+1}'e_{k+1}/(n-k-1)}{y'y/(n-1)}$$

where the subscripts denote the number of regressors. Now

$$
\begin{aligned}
\overline{R}_{k+1}^2 - \overline{R}_k^2 &= \frac{e_k'e_k/(n-k)}{y'y/(n-1)} - \frac{e_{k+1}'e_{k+1}/(n-k-1)}{y'y/(n-1)} \\
&= \frac{n-1}{(n-k)(n-k-1)y'y}\left((n-k-1)e_k'e_k - (n-k)e_{k+1}'e_{k+1}\right)
\end{aligned}
\tag{3.1}
$$

The F-statistic in Eq. (3.44) that contrasts the *RSS* from the restricted and unrestricted regressions is

$$F = \frac{(e_k'e_k - e_{k+1}'e_{k+1})/1}{e_{k+1}'e_{k+1}/(n-k-1)} \tag{3.2}$$

and so $F > 1$ iff

$$
\begin{aligned}
(n-k-1)(e_k'e_k - e_{k+1}'e_{k+1}) &> e_{k+1}'e_{k+1} \\
(n-k-1)e_k'e_k &> (n-k)e_{k+1}'e_{k+1}
\end{aligned}
\tag{3.3}
$$

Therefore (3.1) and (3.3) show that $\overline{R}_{k+1}^2 > \overline{R}_k^2$ iff $F > 1$.

To show

$$r_{k+1}^2 = \frac{F}{F + df} = \frac{t^2}{t^2 + df} \tag{3.4}$$

we generalize the decomposition in Eq. (3.16) to

$$R_{k+1}^2 = R_k^2 + r_{k+1}^2(1 - R_k^2)$$

This says that the variation in Y explained by $(k+1)$ regressors is the sum of the part explained by the first k regressors and the part that the $(k+1)$-th regressor can explain which the first k regressors could not explain. Solving for r_{k+1}^2 yields

$$r_{k+1}^2 = \frac{R_{k+1}^2 - R_k^2}{1 - R_k^2} = \frac{e_k'e_k - e_{k+1}'e_{k+1}}{e_k'e_k} = 1 - \frac{e_{k+1}'e_{k+1}}{e_k'e_k} \tag{3.5}$$

After some algebra, we can rewrite (3.2) as

$$\frac{e_{k+1}'e_{k+1}}{e_k'e_k} = \frac{n-k-1}{F+n-k-1} = \frac{df}{F+df}$$

Substituting this expression into (3.5) yields

$$r_{k+1}^2 = \frac{F}{F + df}$$

The last equality in (3.4) follows since the F-distribution with one degrees of freedom in the numerator is equivalent to the square of the t-distribution with the denominator degrees of freedom (Eq. (1.59)).

3.19.   Rewrite the regression as

$$\begin{aligned} Y &= \beta_1 + \beta_2 X_2 + \beta_3(X_3 - X_2) + u \\ &= \beta_1 + (\beta_2 - \beta_3)X_2 + \beta_3 X_3 + u \end{aligned}$$

This is the regression the research assistant estimated. Comparing the coefficients, we have

$$b_2 = a_2 + b_3 = a_2 + a_3 = -0.04$$

To carry out the test, we need an estimate of the variance of b_2

$$\begin{aligned} var(b_2) &= var(a_2 + a_3) \\ &= var(a_2) + 2cov(a_2, a_3) + var(a_3) \\ &= \left(\frac{-0.24}{1.8}\right)^2 + 2 \times 0.003 + \left(\frac{0.20}{2.3}\right)^2 \\ &= 0.0313 \end{aligned}$$

The test statistic for the significance of β_2 is then

$$t = \frac{b_2}{s.e.(b_2)} = \frac{-0.04}{\sqrt{0.0313}} = -0.226$$

This is not significant at conventional significance levels and for any sample size. We cannot reject the hypothesis that average speed has no effect on fatalities.

3.20.

(a) In a three variable problem we have one regressand and two regressors. Since the $X'X$ matrix is 3×3, X includes a constant with $X = [i \; X_2 \; X_3]$. The $(1,1)$ element of $X'X$ gives the sample size as $n = 33$.

(b) In deviation form the regression is

$$y = \beta_2 x_2 + \beta_3 x_3 + u$$

To solve the normal equations we need $X'X$ and $X'y$ in deviation form. But notice from the first row (column) of $X'X$ that the regressors have zero mean. Therefore the lower right 2×2 submatrix of $X'X$ is already in deviation form. Since $\sum(X - \bar{X})(Y - \bar{Y}) = \sum(X - \bar{X})Y = \sum XY$, the lower 2×1 subvector of $X'y$ is also in deviation form. The estimated slope coefficients are thus

$$\begin{bmatrix} b_2 \\ b_3 \end{bmatrix} = \begin{bmatrix} 40 & 20 \\ 20 & 60 \end{bmatrix}^{-1} \begin{bmatrix} 24 \\ 92 \end{bmatrix} = \begin{bmatrix} -0.2 \\ 1.6 \end{bmatrix}$$

and the intercept is

$$b_1 = \overline{Y} - b_2\overline{X}_2 - b_3\overline{X}_3 = \overline{Y} = \frac{132}{33} = 4$$

The estimated regression equation is therefore

$$Y = 4 - 0.2X_2 + 1.6X_3$$

(c) The *RSS* is

$$e'e = y'y - b'X'y = 150 - [-0.2\ 1.6]\begin{bmatrix} 24 \\ 92 \end{bmatrix} = 7.6$$

and the estimated variances of the slope coefficients are

$$var\begin{bmatrix} b_2 \\ b_3 \end{bmatrix} = \frac{e'e}{n-k}\begin{bmatrix} 40 & 20 \\ 20 & 60 \end{bmatrix}^{-1} = \begin{bmatrix} 0.0076 & -0.0025 \\ -0.0025 & 0.0051 \end{bmatrix}$$

The test statistic for the hypothesis $\beta_2 = 0$ is

$$t = \frac{b_2}{s.e.(b_2)} = \frac{-0.2}{\sqrt{0.0076}} = -2.294$$

The critical values are $t_{.975}(30) = 2.042$ and $t_{.995}(30) = 2.750$. Therefore β_2 is significantly different from zero at 5% significance level but not at 1% significance level.

(d) The restricted regression is Y on a constant and X_3. The estimated slope coefficient of this restricted regression is

$$b_* = \frac{x_3'y}{x_3'x_3} = \frac{92}{60} = 1.533$$

with *RSS*

$$e_*'e_* = y'y - b_*'x_3'y = 150 - \frac{92^2}{60} = 8.933$$

The F statistic is

$$F = \frac{(e_*'e_* - e'e)/q}{e'e/(n-k)} = \frac{(8.933 - 7.6)/1}{7.6/30} = 5.262 = t^2$$

The critical values are $F_{.950}(1, 30) = 4.17$ and $F_{.990}(1, 30) = 7.56$.

(e) The point forecast is

$$\widehat{Y}_f = 4 - 0.2 \times (-4) + 1.6 \times 3 = 9.6$$

with variance

$$\begin{aligned} var(\widehat{Y}) &= E(Y - \widehat{Y})^2 \\ &= E[x'(\beta - b) - u]^2 \\ &= x'E(\beta - b)(\beta - b)'x + s^2 \\ &= s^2[x'(X'X)^{-1}x + 1] \\ &= \frac{7.6}{30}\left([-4\ 2]\begin{bmatrix} 0.03 & -0.01 \\ -0.01 & 0.02 \end{bmatrix}\begin{bmatrix} -4 \\ 2 \end{bmatrix} + 1\right) \\ &= 0.436 \end{aligned}$$

Therefore the 95% confidence interval for Y_f is

$$\widehat{Y} \pm t_{.975}(30)\sqrt{var(\widehat{Y})}$$
$$= \quad 9.6 \pm 2.042 \times \sqrt{0.436}$$
$$= \quad 8.252 \quad \text{to} \quad 10.948$$

Since $Y_f = 12$ lies outside the 95% confidence forecast interval, we suspect a change in the underlying relationship.

Chapter 4

4.1. OLS estimates from the 20 observations are

$$b = (X'X)^{-1}X'y = \begin{bmatrix} 2 & 1 \\ 1 & 3 \end{bmatrix}^{-1} \begin{bmatrix} 3 \\ 4 \end{bmatrix} = \begin{bmatrix} 1 \\ 1 \end{bmatrix}$$

with

$$e'e = y'y - b'X'y = 75 - [1\ 1]\begin{bmatrix} 30 \\ 40 \end{bmatrix} = 5$$

The point forecast given $X = 2$ is

$$\widehat{Y} = b_1 + b_2 x_2 = 3$$

with variance

$$
\begin{aligned}
var(\widehat{Y}) &= s^2\left(1 + x'(X'X)^{-1}x\right) \\
&= \frac{5}{20-2}\left(1 + [1\ 2]\begin{bmatrix} 20 & 10 \\ 10 & 30 \end{bmatrix}^{-1}\begin{bmatrix} 1 \\ 2 \end{bmatrix}\right) \\
&= 0.317
\end{aligned}
$$

The test statistic for the null hypothesis that the parameters have not changed is

$$t = \frac{\widehat{Y} - Y}{s.e.(\widehat{Y})} = \frac{3-4}{\sqrt{0.317}} = -1.776$$

The 5% critical value is $t_{.975}(18) = 2.101$ and we cannot reject the hypothesis of parameter constancy (at 5% significance level).

Alternatively, we can contrast the RSS from the restricted ($e'_* e_*$) and unrestricted ($e'e$) regressions. The RSS from the unrestricted regression is the sum of the RSS from the two sub-samples. But the second sub-sample has only one observation to estimate two parameters so we have a perfect fit with $e'_2 e_2 = 0$. Therefore the RSS from the unrestricted regression is

$$e'e = e'_1 e_1 + e'_2 e_2 = 5 + 0 = 5$$

The RSS from the restricted regression comes from fitting all 21 observations. The design matrices are now

$$X'X = \begin{bmatrix} 21 & 12 \\ 12 & 34 \end{bmatrix}, \qquad X'y = \begin{bmatrix} 34 \\ 48 \end{bmatrix}, \qquad y'y = 91$$

The restricted RSS is

$$
\begin{aligned}
e'_* e_* &= y'y - y'X(X'X)^{-1}X'y \\
&= 91 - [34\ 48] \begin{bmatrix} 21 & 12 \\ 12 & 34 \end{bmatrix}^{-1} \begin{bmatrix} 34 \\ 48 \end{bmatrix} \\
&= 5.877
\end{aligned}
$$

Therefore the forecast Chow test in Eq. (4.15) is

$$
F = \frac{(e'_* e_* - e'_1 e_1)/n_2}{e'_1 e_1/(n_1 - k)} = \frac{(5.877 - 5)/1}{5/18} = 3.157 = t^2
$$

Note that the numerator degrees of freedom is n_2, not k. The 5% critical value is $F_{.950}(1, 18) = 4.41$ and we cannot reject the hypothesis of parameter constancy (at 5% significance level).

4.2.   To test for the presence of seasonality we test the joint significance of the three seasonal dummy variables. The restricted RSS is $e'_* e_* = 18.48$, while the unrestricted RSS is

$$
e'e = TSS - ESS = (109.6 + 18.48) - 114.8 = 13.28
$$

The F test contrasting the restricted and unrestricted RSS is

$$
F = \frac{(e'_* e_* - e'e)/q}{e'e/(n - k)} = \frac{(18.48 - 13.28)/3}{13.28/69} = 9.006
$$

The 5% critical value is $F_{.950}(3, 70) = 2.74$ and we reject the hypothesis of no seasonality (at 5% significance level).

There are two ways to test for parameter constancy over the two sub-samples. The Chow forecast test in Eq. (4.15) is[1]

$$
F = \frac{(e'_* e_* - e'_1 e_1)/n_2}{e'_1 e_1/(n_1 - k)} = \frac{(18.48 - 9.32)/32}{9.32/(44 - 4)} = 1.229
$$

The 5% critical value is $F_{.950}(30, 40) = 1.74$ and we cannot reject the hypothesis of parameter constancy (at 5% significance level).

The break-point Chow test (using $e'e = e'_1 e_1 + e'_2 e_2$) is

$$
F = \frac{(e'_* e_* - e'e)/k}{e'e/(n - 2k)} = \frac{(18.48 - (9.32 + 7.46))/4}{(9.32 + 7.46)/68} = 1.722
$$

The 5% critical value is $F_{.950}(4, 70) = 2.50$ and we cannot reject the hypothesis of parameter constancy (at 5% significance level).

4.3.   The point forecasts are

$$
\begin{aligned}
\widehat{Q}_1 &= 70 - 0.01\widehat{P}_1 + 0.2\widehat{Y}_1 - 1.5 &=& 87.4 \\
\widehat{Q}_2 &= 70 - 0.01\widehat{P}_2 + 0.2\widehat{Y}_2 + 3.6 &=& 92.84 \\
\widehat{Q}_3 &= 70 - 0.01\widehat{P}_3 + 0.2\widehat{Y}_3 + 4.7 &=& 94.28 \\
\widehat{Q}_4 &= 70 - 0.01\widehat{P}_4 + 0.2\widehat{Y}_4 &=& 89.46
\end{aligned}
$$

---

[1] One can also do the Chow "back-forecast" test

$$
F = \frac{(e'_* e_* - e'_2 e_2)/n_1}{e'_2 e_2/(n_2 - k)}
$$

The regression with a constant, S_2, S_3, S_4 is

$$Q = \alpha_1 + \alpha_2 S_2 + \alpha_3 S_3 + \alpha_4 S_4 + \beta P + \gamma Y$$

Rewrite this equation using the identity $S_4 = i - S_1 - S_2 - S_3$ as

$$
\begin{aligned}
Q &= \alpha_1 + \alpha_2 S_2 + \alpha_3 S_3 + \alpha_4(i - S_1 - S_2 - S_3) + \beta P + \gamma Y \\
&= \alpha_1 + \alpha_4 - \alpha_4 S_1 + (\alpha_2 - \alpha_4)S_2 + (\alpha_3 - \alpha_4)S_3 + \beta P + \gamma Y
\end{aligned}
$$

This is the original regression. Comparing the coefficients, we have

$$
\begin{cases}
\alpha_1 + \alpha_4 &= 70 \\
\alpha_4 &= 1.5 \\
\alpha_2 - \alpha_4 &= 3.6 \\
\alpha_3 - \alpha_4 &= 4.7 \\
\beta &= -0.01 \\
\gamma &= 0.2
\end{cases}
\quad \text{or} \quad
\begin{cases}
\alpha_1 &= 68.5 \\
\alpha_2 &= 5.1 \\
\alpha_3 &= 6.2 \\
\alpha_4 &= 1.5 \\
\beta &= -0.01 \\
\gamma &= 0.2
\end{cases}
$$

Therefore the estimated regression equation will be

$$Q = 68.5 + 5.1 S_2 + 6.2 S_3 + 1.5 S_4 - 0.01P + 0.2Y$$

When we include all quarterly dummy variables without a constant, the regression is

$$
\begin{aligned}
Q &= \alpha_1 S_1 + \alpha_2 S_2 + \alpha_3 S_3 + \alpha_4 S_4 + \beta P + \gamma Y \\
&= \alpha_1 S_1 + \alpha_2 S_2 + \alpha_3 S_3 + \alpha_4(i - S_1 - S_2 - S_3) + \beta P + \gamma Y \\
&= \alpha_4 + (\alpha_1 - \alpha_4)S_1 + (\alpha_2 - \alpha_4)S_2 + (\alpha_3 - \alpha_4)S_3 + \beta P + \gamma Y
\end{aligned}
$$

Comparing the coefficients with the original regression we now have

$$\alpha_1 = 68.5, \quad \alpha_2 = 73.6, \quad \alpha_3 = 74.7, \quad \alpha_4 = 70, \quad \beta = -0.01, \quad \gamma = 0.2$$

and so the estimated regression equation will be

$$Q = 68.5 S_1 + 73.6 S_2 + 74.7 S_3 + 70 S_4 - 0.01P + 0.2Y$$

4.4. Use the identity $i = E_1 + E_2 + E_3$ to rewrite the regression as

$$
\begin{aligned}
Y &= \alpha_1 i + \gamma_2 E_2 + \gamma_3 E_3 + u \\
&= \alpha_1(E_1 + E_2 + E_3) + \gamma_2 E_2 + \gamma_3 E_3 + u \\
&= \alpha_1 E_1 + (\alpha_1 + \gamma_2)E_2 + (\alpha_1 + \gamma_3)E_3 + u
\end{aligned}
$$

Since the three dummy variables E_1, E_2, E_3 are mutually exclusive and exhaustive, they are orthogonal to each other. Therefore the coefficient on each regressor will be the same as the coefficient from regressing Y on each dummy variable alone. Thus

$$
\begin{cases}
a_1 &= \sum Y E_1 / \sum E_1^2 = \sum_1 Y/n_1 = \overline{Y}_1 \\
a_1 + c_2 &= \sum Y E_2 / \sum E_2^2 = \sum_2 Y/n_2 = \overline{Y}_2 \\
a_1 + c_3 &= \sum Y E_3 / \sum E_3^2 = \sum_3 Y/n_3 = \overline{Y}_3
\end{cases}
$$

or

$$
\begin{cases}
a_1 &= \overline{Y}_1 \\
c_2 &= \overline{Y}_2 - \overline{Y}_1 \\
c_3 &= \overline{Y}_3 - \overline{Y}_1
\end{cases}
$$

4.5. Each equation can be estimated without actually re-running the regression by following the same steps as in Problem 4.3.

```
. reg Y E1 E2 E3 S2, noc

    Source |       SS       df       MS                Number of obs =      13
-----------+------------------------------            F(  4,     9) =  160.04
     Model |    2774.00        4    693.50            Prob > F      =  0.0000
  Residual |      39.00        9  4.33333333          R-square      =  0.9861
-----------+------------------------------            Adj R-square  =  0.9800
     Total |    2813.00       13  216.384615          Root MSE      =  2.0817


         Y |    Coef.   Std. Err.       t    P>|t|     [95% Conf. Interval]
-----------+------------------------------------------------------------------
        E1 |        9   1.040833     8.647   0.000     6.645472    11.35453
        E2 |       13   1.192424    10.902   0.000     10.30255    15.69745
        E3 |     22.5   1.192424    18.869   0.000     19.80255    25.19745
        S2 |       -2   1.163687    -1.719   0.120    -4.632442     .6324421
------------------------------------------------------------------------------


. reg Y E1 E2 S2

    Source |       SS       df       MS                Number of obs =      13
-----------+------------------------------            F(  3,     9) =   32.17
     Model |  418.230769        3  139.410256         Prob > F      =  0.0000
  Residual |      39.00        9  4.33333333          R-square      =  0.9147
-----------+------------------------------            Adj R-square  =  0.8863
     Total |  457.230769       12  38.1025641         Root MSE      =  2.0817


         Y |    Coef.   Std. Err.       t    P>|t|     [95% Conf. Interval]
-----------+------------------------------------------------------------------
        E1 |    -13.5   1.401264    -9.634   0.000    -16.66988   -10.33012
        E2 |     -9.5    1.47196    -6.454   0.000    -12.82981   -6.170195
        S2 |       -2   1.163687    -1.719   0.120    -4.632442     .6324421
     _cons |     22.5   1.192424    18.869   0.000     19.80255    25.19745
------------------------------------------------------------------------------
```

The estimated equations are

$$Y = 9E_1 + 13E_2 + 22.5E_3 - 2S_2$$
$$Y = 22.5 - 13.5E_1 - 9.5E_2 - 2S_2$$

The mean values should be identical to those in Table 4.5.

4.6.   The regression estimated in the text is

$$Y = 10 + 3E_2 + 11E_3 - 4.5S_2 + 2.5E_2S_2 + 5.5E_3S_2$$

Suppose instead we regress Y on E_1, E_2, E_3 and S_1. There are six possible combinations of interaction terms. But interaction terms within the same category E_1E_2, E_1E_3, E_2E_3 vanish since they are orthogonal to each other. This leaves three cross interaction terms with a total of seven regressors. But these seven regressors cannot be lineary independent. (Note that the original regression has only six regressors). For example,

$$E_1S_1 = (i - E_2 - E_3)S_1 = S_1 - E_2S_1 - E_3S_1$$

so we have to drop one of the three cross interaction terms to avoid perfect collinearity.

```
. reg Y E1 E2 E3 S1 E2S1 E3S1, noc
```

Source	SS	df	MS		
Model	2790.50	6	465.083333		
Residual	22.50	7	3.21428571		
Total	2813.00	13	216.384615		

Number of obs = 13
F(6, 7) = 144.69
Prob > F = 0.0000
R-square = 0.9920
Adj R-square = 0.9851
Root MSE = 1.7928

Y	Coef.	Std. Err.	t	P>|t|	[95% Conf. Interval]
E1	5.5	1.267731	4.338	0.003	2.502292 8.497708
E2	11	1.267731	8.677	0.000	8.002292 13.99771
E3	22	1.267731	17.354	0.000	19.00229 24.99771
S1	4.5	1.636634	2.750	0.029	.6299751 8.370025
E2S1	-2.5	2.427521	-1.030	0.337	-8.240175 3.240175
E3S1	-5.5	2.427521	-2.266	0.058	-11.24017 .2401745

If we drop E_1S_1, the estimated regression is (again we can obtain these estimates without actually re-running the regression)

$$Y = 5.5E_1 + 11E_2 + 22E_3 + 4.5S_1 - 2.5E_2S_1 - 5.5E_3S_1$$

The estimated mean incomes should be the same as those in Table 4.6.

4.7. This is an application of the Chow test to cross-sectional data. There are several ways to carry out the test. One is to do the "break-point" Chow test by comparing the RSS from the restricted and unrestricted regressions. (Note: D is a dummy variable indicating an increase in income.)

```
. sort D

. by D: reg Y X
```

-> D=   0

Source	SS	df	MS		
Model	1806.00676	1	1806.00676		
Residual	57.1932432	3	19.0644144		
Total	1863.20	4	465.80		

Number of obs = 5
F(1, 3) = 94.73
Prob > F = 0.0023
R-square = 0.9693
Adj R-square = 0.9591
Root MSE = 4.3663

Y	Coef.	Std. Err.	t	P>|t|	[95% Conf. Interval]
X	.6986486	.0717812	9.733	0.002	.4702088 .9270885
_cons	16.76216	8.8323	1.898	0.154	-11.34616 44.87048

-> D=   1

Source	SS	df	MS		
Model	4621.52814	1	4621.52814		
Residual	247.900429	5	49.5800858		
Total	4869.42857	6	811.571429		

Number of obs = 7
F(1, 5) = 93.21
Prob > F = 0.0002
R-square = 0.9491
Adj R-square = 0.9389
Root MSE = 7.0413

```
----------------------------------------------------------------
      Y |    Coef.   Std. Err.      t    P>|t|    [95% Conf. Interval]
---------+------------------------------------------------------
      X |  .7452361   .0771889    9.655  0.000    .5468157   .9436564
  _cons |  10.30644   12.20289    0.845  0.437   -21.06209   41.67496
----------------------------------------------------------------

. reg Y X

  Source |       SS       df       MS              Number of obs =      12
---------+------------------------------          F(  1,   10) =  263.66
   Model |  8199.03074    1   8199.03074          Prob > F     =  0.0000
Residual |  310.969256   10   31.0969256          R-square     =  0.9635
---------+------------------------------          Adj R-square =  0.9598
   Total |    8510.00    11   773.636364          Root MSE     =  5.5765

----------------------------------------------------------------
      Y |    Coef.   Std. Err.      t    P>|t|    [95% Conf. Interval]
---------+------------------------------------------------------
      X |   .728479   .0448636   16.238  0.000    .6285166   .8284414
  _cons |  13.01294   6.483921    2.007  0.073   -1.434131   27.46002
----------------------------------------------------------------
```

The test statistic for the null hypothesis that the two class of families have the same consumption function is

$$F = \frac{(e'_* e_* - e'e)/k}{e'e/(n-2k)} = \frac{(310.969 - (57.193 + 247.900))/2}{(57.193 + 247.900)/8} = 0.077$$

This is not significant at any conventional significance levels. We cannot reject the hypothesis of same consumption behavior.

Alternatively, one can use the "forecast" Chow test and compare the actual and fitted values for either sub-sample. There are two possibilities. If we use the non-asterisk families to forecast the asterisk families, the test statistics is

$$F = \frac{(e'_* e_* - e'_1 e_1)/n_2}{e'_1 e_1/(n_1 - k)} = \frac{(310.969 - 57.193)/7}{57.193/(5-2)} = 1.902$$

The 5% critical value is $F_{.950}(7,3) = 8.88$ and we cannot reject the hypothesis of same consumption behavior (at 5% significance level). If we use the asterisk families to forecast the non-asterisk families, the test statistics is

$$F = \frac{(e'_* e_* - e'_2 e_2)/n_1}{e'_2 e_2/(n_2 - k)} = \frac{(310.969 - 247.900)/5}{247.900/(7-2)} = 0.254$$

The 5% critical value is $F_{.950}(5,5) = 5.05$ and we cannot reject the hypothesis of same consumption behavior (at 5% significance level). In this data all three tests reject the null hypothesis but in general the three tests may give conflicting results.

If we want to test whether the marginal propensity to consume (the slope coefficient) differs between the two class, we can run the regression in Eq. (4.40)

$$Y = \alpha + \beta X + \gamma D + \delta(XD) + u$$

and test whether $\delta = 0$.

```
. reg Y X D XD

  Source |       SS        df       MS              Number of obs =      12
---------+------------------------------            F(  3,    8) =   71.71
   Model | 8204.90633        3   2734.96878         Prob > F     =  0.0000
Residual | 305.093672        8   38.1367091         R-square     =  0.9641
---------+------------------------------            Adj R-square =  0.9507
   Total |    8510.00       11   773.636364         Root MSE     =  6.1755


---------------------------------------------------------------------------
       Y |    Coef.   Std. Err.       t     P>|t|     [95% Conf. Interval]
---------+-----------------------------------------------------------------
       X |  .6986486   .1015245     6.882   0.000    .4645328    .9327645
       D | -6.455724   16.44969    -0.392   0.705   -44.38878    31.47733
      XD |  .0465874   .1220253     0.382   0.713   -.2348034    .3279782
   _cons |  16.76216   12.49205     1.342   0.216   -12.04455    45.56888
---------------------------------------------------------------------------
```

The coefficient on the interaction term is not significantly different from zero at conventional significance levels. We cannot reject the hypothesis that the marginal propensity to consume is the same.

4.8. Note that the RSS can be calculated as

$$
\begin{aligned}
e_*'e_* &= (n-k)s^2 = 0.0508 \\
e_1'e_1 &= (n_1-k)s_1^2 = 0.0356 \\
e_2'e_2 &= (n_2-k)s_2^2 = 0.0076 \\
e'e &= e_1'e_1 + e_2'e_2 = 0.0432
\end{aligned}
$$

There are two ways to carry out the test. The forecast Chow test is

$$ F = \frac{(e_*'e_* - e_1'e_1)/n_2}{e_1'e_1/(n_1-k)} = \frac{(.0508 - .0356)/19}{.0356/(20-3)} = .382 $$

The 5% critical value is $F_{.950}(20, 17) = 2.23$. We cannot reject the hypothesis that the production functions are the same over the two periods (at 5% significance level).

The break-point Chow test is

$$ F = \frac{(e_*'e_* - e'e)/k}{e'e/(n-2k)} = \frac{(.0508 - .0432)/3}{.0432/(39-6)} = 1.935 $$

The 5% critical value is $F_{.950}(3, 35) = 2.88$. Again we cannot reject the hypothesis that the production functions are the same over the two periods (at 5% significance level).

4.9. The RSS can be obtained as

$$ e'e = y'y - b'X'y = y'y - y'X(X'X)^{-1}X'y $$

The unrestricted RSS are then

$$ e_1'e_1 = 30 - [10\ 20]\begin{bmatrix} 20 & 20 \\ 20 & 25 \end{bmatrix}^{-1}\begin{bmatrix} 10 \\ 20 \end{bmatrix} = 5 $$

$$ e_2'e_2 = 24 - [8\ 20]\begin{bmatrix} 10 & 10 \\ 10 & 20 \end{bmatrix}^{-1}\begin{bmatrix} 8 \\ 20 \end{bmatrix} = 3.2 $$

To get the restricted *RSS* we need the design matrix for whole sample.

$$X'_* X_* = [X'_1 \ X'_2] \begin{bmatrix} X_1 \\ X_2 \end{bmatrix} = X'_1 X_1 + X'_2 X_2$$

$$= \begin{bmatrix} 20 & 20 \\ 20 & 25 \end{bmatrix} + \begin{bmatrix} 10 & 10 \\ 10 & 20 \end{bmatrix} = \begin{bmatrix} 30 & 30 \\ 30 & 45 \end{bmatrix}$$

$$X'_* y_* = [X'_1 \ X'_2] \begin{bmatrix} y_1 \\ y_2 \end{bmatrix} = X'_1 y_1 + X'_2 y_2$$

$$= \begin{bmatrix} 10 \\ 20 \end{bmatrix} + \begin{bmatrix} 8 \\ 20 \end{bmatrix} = \begin{bmatrix} 18 \\ 40 \end{bmatrix}$$

$$y'_* y_* = y'_1 y_1 + y'_2 y_2 = 54$$

and the restricted *RSS* is

$$e'_* e_* = 54 - [18 \ 40] \begin{bmatrix} 30 & 30 \\ 30 & 45 \end{bmatrix}^{-1} \begin{bmatrix} 18 \\ 40 \end{bmatrix} = 10.933$$

The break-point Chow test is

$$F = \frac{(e'_* e_* - e'_1 e_1 - e'_2 e_2)/k}{(e'_1 e_1 + e'_2 e_2)/(n - 2k)} = \frac{(10.933 - 5 - 3.2)/2}{(5 + 3.2)/26} = 4.333$$

The 5% critical value is $F_{.950}(2, 26) = 3.37$. We reject the hypothesis that urban and rural areas have the same structure (at 5% significance level).

If we use the urban data to forecast the rural data, the Chow forecast test is

$$F = \frac{(e'_* e_* - e'_1 e_1)/n_2}{e'_1 e_1/(n_1 - k)} = \frac{(10.933 - 5)/10}{5/(20 - 2)} = 2.136$$

The 5% critical value is $F_{.950}(10, 18) = 2.41$ and we cannot reject the hypothesis that urban and rural areas have the same structure (at 5% significance level).

If we use the rural data to forecast the urban data, the Chow forecast test is

$$F = \frac{(e'_* e_* - e'_2 e_2)/n_1}{e'_2 e_2/(n_2 - k)} = \frac{(10.933 - 3.2)/20}{3.2/(10 - 2)} = 0.967$$

This is not significant at conventional levels and we cannot reject the hypothesis that urban and rural areas have the same structure.

4.10.　　The unrestricted *RSS* is

$$e'e = (n_1 - k)s_1^2 + (n_2 - k)s_2^2 + (n_3 - k)s_3^2 = 26 + 42 + 15 = 83$$

and the restricted *RSS* is

$$e'_* e_* = (n - k)s^2 = 254 \times 0.38 = 96.52.$$

The "break-point" Chow test is (be careful about the degrees of freedom)

$$F = \frac{(e'_* e_* - e'e)/2k}{e'e/(n - 3k)} = \frac{(96.52 - 83)/4}{83/250} = 10.181$$

This is significant at any conventional significance levels and we reject the hypothesis that all income groups have the same expenditure function.

To test constancy of the slope coefficient (elasticity), we need information from the restricted regression. This can be done by regressing log expenditure on log income and a set of dummy variables indicating each income group.

To test whether the overall income elasticity is 0.10, we can carry out the t test

$$t = \frac{b - 0.10}{\sqrt{s^2 (x'x)^{-1}}} = \frac{0.07 - 0.10}{\sqrt{0.38/(256 \times 24)}} = 3.893$$

This is significant at any conventional significance levels and we reject the hypothesis $\beta = 0.10$.

Chapter 5

5.1.

$$
\begin{array}{rclclcl}
E(y) & = & \sum y f(y) & = & 1f(1) + 0f(0) & = & \theta \\
E(y^2) & = & \sum y^2 f(y) & = & 1f(1) + 0f(0) & = & \theta \\
var(y) & = & E(y^2) - (E(y))^2 & = & \theta(1-\theta) &
\end{array}
$$

To find the MLE of θ, write down the likelihood function

$$
\begin{array}{rcl}
L & = & f(y_1)f(y_2)\cdots f(y_n) \\
& = & \theta^{y_1}(1-\theta)^{(1-y_1)}\theta^{y_2}(1-\theta)^{(1-y_2)}\cdots\theta^{y_n}(1-\theta)^{(1-y_n)} \\
& = & \theta^{\sum y}(1-\theta)^{(n-\sum y)} \\
\ell & = & \ln L \\
& = & \sum y \ln \theta + (n - \sum y)\ln(1-\theta)
\end{array}
$$

The first order condition is

$$
\frac{\partial \ell}{\partial \theta} = \frac{\sum y}{\theta} - \frac{n - \sum y}{1-\theta} = 0
$$

Solving for θ yields the MLE

$$
\widehat{\theta} = \frac{\sum y}{n}
$$

This is the sample proportion of success. The mean and variance of $\widehat{\theta}$ are

$$
E(\widehat{\theta}) = E\left(\frac{\sum y}{n}\right) = \frac{n\theta}{n} = \theta
$$

$$
E(\widehat{\theta}^2) = E\left[\left(\frac{\sum y}{n}\right)^2\right] = \frac{n\theta + n(n-1)\theta^2}{n^2} = \frac{\theta + (n-1)\theta^2}{n}
$$

$$
var(\widehat{\theta}) = E(\widehat{\theta}^2) - \left(E(\widehat{\theta})\right)^2 = \frac{\theta + (n-1)\theta^2}{n} - \theta^2 = \frac{\theta(1-\theta)}{n}
$$

$\widehat{\theta}$ is an unbiased and consistent estimator of θ.

Evaluating the information matrix by the outer product of the gradient (in this case a scalar) yields

$$
I(\theta) = E\left[\left(\frac{\partial \ell}{\partial \theta}\right)^2\right]
$$

$$
\begin{aligned}
&= E\left[\left(\frac{\sum y}{\theta} - \frac{n - \sum y}{1 - \theta}\right)^2\right] \\
&= E\left(\frac{(\sum y)^2}{\theta^2} - \frac{2\left(n\sum y - (\sum y)^2\right)}{\theta(1-\theta)} + \frac{n^2 - 2n\sum y + (\sum y)^2}{(1-\theta)^2}\right) \\
&= \frac{n\theta + n(n-1)\theta^2}{\theta^2} - \frac{2n^2\theta - 2\left(n\theta + n(n-1)\theta^2\right)}{\theta(1-\theta)} + \frac{n^2 - 2n^2\theta + n\theta + n(n-1)\theta^2}{(1-\theta)^2} \\
&= \frac{n}{\theta(1-\theta)}
\end{aligned}
$$

Alternatively, evaluating the information matrix by the negative of the Hessian yields

$$
\begin{aligned}
I(\theta) &= -E\left(\frac{\partial^2 \ell}{\partial \theta^2}\right) \\
&= E\left(\frac{\sum y}{\theta^2} + \frac{n - \sum y}{(1-\theta)^2}\right) \\
&= \frac{n\theta}{\theta^2} + \frac{n - n\theta}{(1-\theta)^2} \\
&= \frac{n}{\theta(1-\theta)}
\end{aligned}
$$

As in this example, evaluating the negative of the Hessian is usually analytically more tractable than evaluating the outer product of the gradient. (This is not necessarily the case when evaluating the information matrix numerically.) The asymptotic variance is the inverse of the information matrix. In this case the exact finite sample variance and the asymptotic variance of the MLE are the same; in some cases the exact finite sample distribution of the MLE is not available.

5.2.   The likelihood function is

$$
\begin{aligned}
L &= f(x_1)f(x_2)\cdots f(x_n) \\
&= \alpha^{-n} \\
\ell &= \ln L \\
&= -n\ln\alpha
\end{aligned}
$$

Notice that the log likelihood is monotonically decreasing in α. Therefore the maximum of l is attained at the minimum of α, a corner solution. (Recall that the first order condition works only when we have an interior solution.) But what is the range of α? The trick is to read the condition $0 < x_i < \alpha$ not as a condition on x but as a condition on α: α must be greater than any sample observation x_i. This implies that α cannot be smaller than the largest sample observation. Thus

$$
\widehat{\alpha} = \min\alpha = \max x_i
$$

The MLE of α is the largest observation in the sample.

Is $\widehat{\alpha}$ an unbiased estimator of α? To calculate the expectation of $\widehat{\alpha}$, we need the distribution of $\max x_i$.

$$
\begin{aligned}
F_{\max}(x) &= \Pr(\max x_i < x) \\
&= \Pr(x_1 < x)\Pr(x_2 < x)\cdots \Pr(x_n < x) \\
&= (x/\alpha)^n
\end{aligned}
$$

The density function of max x_i is then

$$f_{\max}(x) = \frac{dF}{dx} = n\alpha^{-n}x^{(n-1)}$$

and the expected value of $\widehat{\alpha}$ is

$$E(\widehat{\alpha}) = \int_0^\alpha x f_{\max}(x)dx = \frac{n}{n+1}\alpha$$

The MLE is biased by a factor of $n/(n+1)$, which tends to 1 as $n \to \infty$.

5.3. Express p^* in terms of p as

$$p^* = \frac{s+1}{n+2} = \frac{s/n + 1/n}{1 + 2/n} = \frac{p}{1 + 2/n} + \frac{1/n}{1 + 2/n}$$

From Problem 5.1 $E(p) = \theta$ and $var(p) = \theta(1-\theta)/n$ so that

$$
\begin{aligned}
E(p^*) &= \frac{E(p)}{1 + 2/n} + \frac{1/n}{1 + 2/n} \\
&= \frac{\theta}{1 + 2/n} + \frac{1/n}{1 + 2/n} \to \theta \quad \text{as } n \to \infty
\end{aligned}
$$

$$
\begin{aligned}
var(p^*) &= \frac{var(p)}{(1 + 2/n)^2} \\
&= \frac{\theta(1-\theta)}{n(1 + 2/n)^2} \to 0 \quad \text{as } n \to \infty
\end{aligned}
$$

Since convergence in quadratic mean implies convergence in probability, p^* is a consistent estimator of θ. Notice that although p^* is biased, it has smaller variance than p. It is not clear which has a smaller mean squared error (it depends on the parameter θ).

5.4. The likelihood function (with sample size n) is

$$
\begin{aligned}
L &= f(x_1)f(x_2)\cdots f(x_n) \\
&= \frac{1}{\theta}e^{-x_1/\theta}\frac{1}{\theta}e^{-x_2/\theta}\cdots\frac{1}{\theta}e^{-x_n/\theta} \\
&= \theta^{-n}e^{-\sum x/\theta} \\
\ell &= \ln L \\
&= -n\ln\theta - \frac{\sum x}{\theta}
\end{aligned}
$$

The first order condition is

$$\frac{\partial \ell}{\partial \theta} = -\frac{n}{\theta} + \frac{\sum x}{\theta^2} = 0$$

Solving for θ yields the ML *estimator*

$$\widehat{\theta} = \frac{\sum x}{n} = \overline{x}$$

which is the sample mean. For the sample of this problem, the ML *estimate* is then $\widehat{\theta} = 2$.

5.5. The problem is to maximize

$$
\begin{aligned}
\ell^* &= \ell - \mu'(R\beta - r) \\
&= -\frac{n}{2}\ln 2\pi - \frac{n}{2}\ln\sigma^2 - \frac{1}{2\sigma^2}(y - X\beta)'(y - X\beta) - \mu'(R\beta - r)
\end{aligned}
$$

with respect to β, σ^2, μ. The first order condition with respect to β is

$$
\frac{\partial\ell^*}{\partial\beta} = (X'y - X'Xb_*)/\sigma_*^2 - R'\mu = 0
$$

The trick is to pre-multiply both sides by $R(X'X)^{-1}$ and solve for μ

$$
\begin{aligned}
R(X'X)^{-1}R'\mu &= R(X'X)^{-1}(X'y - X'Xb_*)/\sigma_*^2 \\
\mu &= [R(X'X)^{-1}R']^{-1}R\left((X'X)^{-1}X'y - b_*\right)/\sigma_*^2 \\
&= [R(X'X)^{-1}R']^{-1}(Rb - Rb_*)/\sigma_*^2 \\
&= [R(X'X)^{-1}R']^{-1}(Rb - r)/\sigma_*^2
\end{aligned}
$$

Substitute this back into the first order condition and solve for b_*

$$
\begin{aligned}
(X'y - X'Xb_*)/\sigma_*^2 &= R'[R(X'X)^{-1}R']^{-1}(Rb - r)/\sigma_*^2 \\
b_* &= (X'X)^{-1}X'y - (X'X)^{-1}R'[R(X'X)^{-1}R']^{-1}(Rb - r) \\
&= b - (X'X)^{-1}R'[R(X'X)^{-1}R']^{-1}(Rb - r)
\end{aligned}
$$

5.6. The Lagrangian for restricted least squares is

$$
\mathcal{L} = (y - X\beta)'(y - X\beta) - 2\lambda'(R\beta - r)
$$

The first order condition with respect to β gives

$$
\frac{\partial\mathcal{L}}{\partial\beta} = -2X'(y - Xb_*) - 2R'\lambda = 0
$$

or

$$
\begin{aligned}
X'e_* + R'\lambda &= 0 \\
\begin{bmatrix} i' \\ X'_{-1} \end{bmatrix} e_* + \begin{bmatrix} R'_1 \\ R'_{-1} \end{bmatrix}\lambda &= 0
\end{aligned}
$$

where R'_1 is a $1 \times q$ vector of constraints on the intercept. When there are no restrictions on the intercept, $R_1 = 0$ and the first row of the first order condition reduces to $i'e_* = 0$. Otherwise, the restricted residuals do not necessarily sum to zero.

5.7. The restricted regression is

$$
\begin{aligned}
Y &= \beta_1 + \beta_2 X_2 - X_3 \\
Y + X_3 &= \beta_1 + \beta_2 X_2
\end{aligned}
$$

which can be estimated by regressing $Y + X_3$ on a constant and X_2.

```
. reg Y X2 X3

    Source |      SS       df       MS                Number of obs =       5
-----------+------------------------------            F(  2,    2) =   17.67
     Model |    26.50        2    13.25                Prob > F      =  0.0536
  Residual |     1.50        2      .75                R-square      =  0.9464
-----------+------------------------------            Adj R-square  =  0.8929
     Total |    28.00        4     7.00                Root MSE      =  .86603

------------------------------------------------------------------------------
        Y |     Coef.   Std. Err.       t    P>|t|     [95% Conf. Interval]
-----------+------------------------------------------------------------------
       X2 |       2.5   .8660254     2.887   0.102    -1.226207    6.226207
       X3 |      -1.5   1.369306    -1.095   0.388    -7.39165     4.39165
    _cons |         4   4.47493      0.894   0.466    -15.25407    23.25407
------------------------------------------------------------------------------

. gen lhs = Y+X3

. reg lhs X2

    Source |      SS       df       MS                Number of obs =       5
-----------+------------------------------            F(  1,    3) =   90.75
     Model |    48.40        1    48.40                Prob > F      =  0.0025
  Residual |     1.60        3 .533333333             R-square      =  0.9680
-----------+------------------------------            Adj R-square  =  0.9573
     Total |    50.00        4    12.50                Root MSE      =   .7303

------------------------------------------------------------------------------
      lhs |     Coef.   Std. Err.       t    P>|t|     [95% Conf. Interval]
-----------+------------------------------------------------------------------
       X2 |       2.2   .2309401     9.526   0.002     1.465046    2.934954
    _cons |       2.4   .7659417     3.133   0.052    -.0375683    4.837568
------------------------------------------------------------------------------

. pre res, res

. reg res X2 X3

    Source |      SS       df       MS                Number of obs =       5
-----------+------------------------------            F(  2,    2) =    0.07
     Model | .100000006        2 .050000003           Prob > F      =  0.9375
  Residual | 1.50000003        2 .750000015           R-square      =  0.0625
-----------+------------------------------            Adj R-square  = -0.8750
     Total | 1.60000004        4 .400000009           Root MSE      =  .86603

------------------------------------------------------------------------------
      res |     Coef.   Std. Err.       t    P>|t|     [95% Conf. Interval]
-----------+------------------------------------------------------------------
       X2 |        .3   .8660254     0.346   0.762    -3.426207    4.026207
       X3 |       -.5   1.369306    -0.365   0.750    -6.39165     5.39165
    _cons |       1.6   4.47493      0.358   0.755    -17.65407    20.85407
------------------------------------------------------------------------------
```

The three test statistics are

$$
\begin{aligned}
W &= & n(e_*'e_* - e'e)/e'e   &= & 5(1.6 - 1.5)/1.5   &= & 0.333 \\
LR &= & n \ln(e_*'e_*/e'e)   &= & 5 \ln(1.6/1.5)   &= & 0.323 \\
LM &= & n(e_*'e_* - e'e)/e_*'e_* &= & 5(1.6 - 1.5)/1.6 &= & 0.313
\end{aligned}
$$

None are significant at conventional significance levels. We cannot reject the hypothesis $\beta_3 = -1$, with the caveat that the sample size is too small to apply asymptotic results.

The nR^2 from the auxiliary regression confirms

$$nR^2 = 5 \times 0.0625 = 0.3125 = LM.$$

5.8.   The restricted regression is

$$
\begin{aligned}
Y &= \beta_1 + \beta_2 X_2 - \beta_2 X_3 \\
&= \beta_1 + \beta_2 (X_2 - X_3)
\end{aligned}
$$

which can be estimated by regressing Y on a constant and $X_2 - X_3$.

```
. gen rhs = X2-X3

. reg Y rhs

      Source |       SS       df       MS                  Number of obs =       5
-------------+------------------------------              F( 1,     3) =   21.00
       Model |    24.50        1      24.50                Prob > F      =  0.0195
    Residual |     3.50        3   1.16666667             R-square      =  0.8750
-------------+------------------------------              Adj R-square  =  0.8333
       Total |    28.00        4       7.00               Root MSE      =  1.0801


           Y |    Coef.   Std. Err.      t     P>|t|     [95% Conf. Interval]
-------------+----------------------------------------------------------------
         rhs |      3.5   .7637626     4.583    0.020     1.069366    5.930634
       _cons |       11   1.602082     6.866    0.006      5.90146    16.09854
------------------------------------------------------------------------------


. pre res, res

. reg res X2 X3

      Source |       SS       df       MS                  Number of obs =       5
-------------+------------------------------              F( 2,     2) =    1.33
       Model |     2.00        2       1.00               Prob > F      =  0.4286
    Residual |     1.50        2        .75               R-square      =  0.5714
-------------+------------------------------              Adj R-square  =  0.1429
       Total |     3.50        4       .875               Root MSE      =  .86603


         res |    Coef.   Std. Err.      t     P>|t|     [95% Conf. Interval]
-------------+----------------------------------------------------------------
          X2 |       -1   .8660254    -1.155    0.368    -4.726207    2.726207
          X3 |        2   1.369306     1.461    0.282     -3.89165     7.89165
       _cons |       -7    4.47493    -1.564    0.258    -26.25407    12.25407
------------------------------------------------------------------------------
```

The three test statistics are

$$
\begin{aligned}
W &= n(e'_* e_* - e'e)/e'e &= 5(3.5 - 1.5)/1.5 &= 6.667 \\
LR &= n\ln(e'_* e_*/e'e) &= 5\ln(3.5/1.5) &= 4.236 \\
LM &= n(e'_* e_* - e'e)/e'_* e_* &= 5(3.5 - 1.5)/3.5 &= 2.857
\end{aligned}
$$

The 5% critical value is $\chi^2_{.950}(1) = 3.84$. The W and LR test reject (at 5% significance level) the hypothesis that the two slope coefficients sum to zero, but the LM test does not. Although asymptotically equivalent, the three tests can diverge in finite samples, especially when the sample size is small.

The nR^2 from the auxiliary regression confirms

$$nR^2 = 5 \times 0.5714 = 2.857 = LM.$$

5.9. The matrix of regressors in the second stage regression is

$$\widehat{X} = P_z X$$
$$= Z(Z'Z)^{-1}Z'X$$
$$\left[\widehat{X}_1 \ \widehat{X}_2\right] = \left[Z(Z'Z)^{-1}Z'X_1 \ \ Z(Z'Z)^{-1}Z'X_2\right]$$

We need to show

$$Z(Z'Z)^{-1}Z'X_1 = P_z X_1 = X_1.$$

But this is evident if we recall that P_z is a projection on Z. Since the Z space is spanned by X_1 and Z_1, if we project X_1 on Z it will simply coincide with X_1 itself.

Chapter 6

6.1. The error covariance matrix is

$$E(uu') = \sigma^2 \begin{bmatrix} X_1^2 & & & \\ & X_2^2 & & 0 \\ & & \ddots & \\ 0 & & & X_n^2 \end{bmatrix} = \sigma^2 \Omega$$

The transformation matrix P that satisfies $P'P = \Omega^{-1}$ is then

$$P = \begin{bmatrix} 1/X_1 & & & \\ & 1/X_2 & & 0 \\ & & \ddots & \\ 0 & & & 1/X_n \end{bmatrix}$$

The transformed variables are

$$y_* = Py = \begin{bmatrix} 1/X_1 & & & \\ & 1/X_2 & & 0 \\ & & \ddots & \\ 0 & & & 1/X_n \end{bmatrix} \begin{bmatrix} y_1 \\ y_2 \\ \vdots \\ y_n \end{bmatrix} = \begin{bmatrix} y_1/X_1 \\ y_2/X_2 \\ \vdots \\ y_n/X_n \end{bmatrix}$$

$$X_* = PX = \begin{bmatrix} 1/X_1 & & & \\ & 1/X_2 & & 0 \\ & & \ddots & \\ 0 & & & 1/X_n \end{bmatrix} \begin{bmatrix} 1 & X_1 \\ 1 & X_2 \\ \vdots & \vdots \\ 1 & X_n \end{bmatrix} = \begin{bmatrix} 1/X_1 & 1 \\ 1/X_2 & 1 \\ \vdots & \vdots \\ 1/X_n & 1 \end{bmatrix}$$

Therefore GLS is just OLS of y/X on $1/X$ and a constant. In other words, GLS is weighted LS with the inverse of X as weights. Note that the original slope coefficient will be estimated as the intercept in the transformed regression.

Many regression packages allow to specify the weights as an option. But it is instructive to ask students to carry out GLS by generating the transformed variables.

```
. reg Y X [w=1/X^2]
(analytic weights assumed)
(sum of wgt is   1.3681e+00)

  Source |      SS       df       MS              Number of obs =        5
---------+------------------------------          F( 1,     3) =    27.35
   Model | 18.4213008      1  18.4213008          Prob > F      =   0.0136
Residual |  2.0203109      3  .673436965          R-square      =   0.9012
---------+------------------------------          Adj R-square  =   0.8682
   Total | 20.4416117      4  5.11040292          Root MSE      =   .82063


---------------------------------------------------------------------------
       Y |     Coef.   Std. Err.       t      P>|t|     [95% Conf. Interval]
---------+-----------------------------------------------------------------
       X |  1.649347   .3153554      5.230    0.014      .645745    2.652948
   _cons |  1.218442   .6028682      2.021    0.137    -.7001539    3.137038
---------------------------------------------------------------------------


. gen lhs = Y/X

. gen rhs = 1/X

. reg lhs rhs

  Source |      SS       df       MS              Number of obs =        5
---------+------------------------------          F( 1,     3) =     4.08
   Model | .752692385     1  .752692385           Prob > F      =   0.1365
Residual | .552807662     3  .184269221           R-square      =   0.5766
---------+------------------------------          Adj R-square  =   0.4354
   Total | 1.30550005      4  .326375012           Root MSE      =   .42927


---------------------------------------------------------------------------
     lhs |     Coef.   Std. Err.       t      P>|t|     [95% Conf. Interval]
---------+-----------------------------------------------------------------
     rhs |  1.218442   .6028683      2.021    0.137    -.7001541    3.137038
   _cons |  1.649347   .3153554      5.230    0.014      .645745    2.652948
---------------------------------------------------------------------------
```

6.2.

```
. reg Y X

  Source |      SS       df       MS              Number of obs =        5
---------+------------------------------          F( 1,     3) =   245.00
   Model |    122.50      1     122.50            Prob > F      =   0.0006
Residual |      1.50      3        .50            R-square      =   0.9879
---------+------------------------------          Adj R-square  =   0.9839
   Total |    124.00      4      31.00            Root MSE      =   .70711


---------------------------------------------------------------------------
       Y |     Coef.   Std. Err.       t      P>|t|     [95% Conf. Interval]
---------+-----------------------------------------------------------------
       X |      1.75   .1118034     15.652    0.001     1.394192    2.105808
   _cons |         1   .5477226      1.826    0.165    -.7430976    2.743098
---------------------------------------------------------------------------
```

The correct variance of the OLS estimator under heteroskedasticity is given in Eq. (6.3) as

$$\sigma^2(X'X)^{-1}X'\Omega X(X'X)^{-1}$$

To get an estimate of this covariance matrix, we need an estimate of σ^2. The OLS residuals (which assume homoskedasticity) cannot be used to estimate σ^2. An unbiased estimate of this factor of proportionality is given in Eq. (5.27) as

$$s^2 = (y - Xb_{GLS})'\Omega^{-1}(y - Xb_{GLS})/(n-k) = 4.6454$$

Substitution in Eq. (6.3) gives an estimate of the correct OLS covariance matrix as

$$\sigma^2(X'X)^{-1}X'\Omega X(X'X)^{-1} = \begin{bmatrix} 0.4042 & -0.0685 \\ -0.0685 & 0.0183 \end{bmatrix}$$

with standard errors s.e.$(b_0) = .6357$ and s.e.$(b_1) = .1352$. For this data the correct standard errors are both larger than the incorrect ones. In general there is no way to tell which will be larger (or smaller). The standard errors of the efficient GLS estimators are s.e.$(b_0) = .5721$ and s.e.$(b_1) = .1318$. The incorrect OLS standard errors are smaller than the efficient GLS standard errors.

6.3.

1. Regress y_t on x_t to obtain the OLS residuals $\hat{u}_t$.

2. Regress $\ln \hat{u}_t^2$ on z_t and calculate the fitted values $\hat{\sigma}_t^2 = e^{z_t'a}$.

3. Regress $y_t/\hat{\sigma}_t$ on $x_t/\hat{\sigma}_t$. In other words, FGLS in this case is weighted LS using the inverse of the square root of the estimated variance as weights.

6.4. I use the last 100 observations from CPS88. The White test is

```
. drop if obs<=900
(900 observations deleted)

. reg lnwage grade potexp exp2 union

  Source |       SS       df       MS              Number of obs =     100
---------+------------------------------           F(  4,    95) =   13.64
   Model | 10.3491652      4   2.5872913           Prob > F      =  0.0000
Residual | 18.0146308     95  .189627693           R-squared     =  0.3649
---------+------------------------------           Adj R-squared =  0.3381
   Total | 28.3637961     99   .28650299           Root MSE      =  .43546


---------------------------------------------------------------------------
  lnwage |      Coef.   Std. Err.       t     P>|t|    [95% Conf. Interval]
---------+-----------------------------------------------------------------
   grade |   .0996467   .0209953     4.746    0.000    .0579658    .1413276
  potexp |    .039043   .0128984     3.027    0.003    .0134363    .0646496
    exp2 |  -.0004686   .0002809    -1.668    0.099   -.0010262     .000089
   union |   .2203713   .1000743     2.202    0.030    .0216988    .4190439
   _cons |   .4564348   .2904413     1.572    0.119    -.120164    1.033034
---------------------------------------------------------------------------

. pre res, res

. gen ressq=res^2

. gen white1=grade^2

. gen white2=potexp*exp2
```

```
. gen white3=grade*exp2

. gen white4=potexp*union

. gen white5=exp2^2

. gen white6=grade*potexp

. gen white7=grade*union

. gen white8=exp2*union

. qui reg ressq grade potexp exp2 union white* if obs>900

. dis chiprob(12,_result(1)*_result(7))
.04041912
```

The p-value of the test statistic is marginally significant at 5% level and we reject the hypothesis of homoskedasticity. The two versions of Breusch-Pagan/Godfrey test are

```
. drop if obs<=900
(900 observations deleted)

. qui reg lnwage grade potexp exp2 union

. pre res, res

. gen ressq=res^2

. scalar sigsq=_result(4)/_result(1)

. gen lhs=ressq/sigsq

. qui reg lhs grade potexp union

. dis chiprob(3,_result(2)/2)
.00706022

. reg ressq grade potexp union if obs>900

      Source |       SS       df       MS                  Number of obs =     100
-------------+------------------------------              F(  3,    96) =    3.51
       Model | .725667096      3  .241889032              Prob > F      =  0.0183
    Residual | 6.62299126     96  .068989492              R-squared     =  0.0987
-------------+------------------------------              Adj R-squared =  0.0706
       Total | 7.34865836     99  .074228872              Root MSE      =  .26266

. dis chiprob(3,9.87)
.01970413
```

The $ESS/2$ version has a p-value of .007 and the nR^2 version has a p-value of .0197; both reject the null hypothesis of homoskedasticity (at 5% significance). The Goldfeld-Quandt test is

```
. drop if obs<=900
(900 observations deleted)

. sort potexp

. qui reg lnwage grade potexp exp2 union if _n<=35

. scalar rss1=_result(4)
```

```
. qui reg lnwage grade potexp exp2 union if _n>65

. scalar rss2=_result(4)

. dis fprob(30,30,rss2/rss1)
.20170113
```

The p-value of the ratio of RSS is .2017; in this case we cannot reject the hypothesis of homoskedasticity.

6.5.   By inspecting the data for years of experience in CPS88, I use the partition

$$
\begin{aligned}
\textbf{potexp} \leq 10 && (n_1 = 321) \\
10 < \textbf{potexp} \leq 20 && (n_2 = 277) \\
20 < \textbf{potexp} \leq 30 && (n_3 = 191) \\
30 < \textbf{potexp} && (n_4 = 211)
\end{aligned}
$$

so that each group has approximately the same number of observations. The test of groupwise homoskedasticity is

```
. qui reg lnwage grade potexp exp2 union

. scalar nlogs=_result(1)*log(_result(4)/_result(1))

. qui reg lnwage grade potexp exp2 union if potexp<=10

. scalar nlogs1=_result(1)*log(_result(4)/_result(1))

. qui reg lnwage grade potexp exp2 union if potexp>10 & potexp<=20

. scalar nlogs2=_result(1)*log(_result(4)/_result(1))

. qui reg lnwage grade potexp exp2 union if potexp>20 & potexp<=30

. scalar nlogs3=_result(1)*log(_result(4)/_result(1))

. qui reg lnwage grade potexp exp2 union if potexp>30

. scalar nlogs4=_result(1)*log(_result(4)/_result(1))

. scalar lr=nlogs-nlogs1-nlogs2-nlogs3-nlogs4

. dis chiprob(3,lr)
2.887e-15
```

The LR test statistic in Eq. (6.21) is highly significant and we reject the null hypothesis of groupwise homoskedasticity.

6.6.   We start from the log-likelihood in Eq. (6.16)

$$
\ell = -\frac{n}{2} \ln 2\pi - \frac{1}{2} \ln |V| - \frac{1}{2} u'V^{-1}u
$$

where

$$
V = \sigma_\epsilon^2 \Omega = \sigma_\epsilon^2 P^{-1}(P')^{-1}
$$

with Ω and P defined in Eqs. (6.65) and (6.67). Then

$$
|V| = |\sigma_\epsilon^2 \Omega| = \sigma_\epsilon^{2n} |\Omega| = \frac{\sigma_\epsilon^{2n}}{1 - \varphi^2}
$$

From Eq. (6.59) $u = P^{-1}\epsilon$ and

$$u'V^{-1}u = (P^{-1}\epsilon)'(\sigma_\epsilon^2\Omega)^{-1}P^{-1}\epsilon = \epsilon'(P^{-1})'\Omega^{-1}P^{-1}\epsilon/\sigma_\epsilon^2 = \epsilon'\epsilon/\sigma_\epsilon^2$$

Substituting these results into the log likelihood yields

$$
\begin{aligned}
\ell &= -\frac{n}{2}\ln 2\pi - \frac{1}{2}\ln\left(\frac{\sigma_\epsilon^{2n}}{1-\varphi^2}\right) - \frac{1}{2\sigma_\epsilon^2}\epsilon'\epsilon \\
&= -\frac{n}{2}\ln 2\pi - \frac{n}{2}\ln\sigma_\epsilon^2 + \frac{1}{2}\ln(1-\varphi^2) - \frac{1}{2\sigma_\epsilon^2}\epsilon'\epsilon
\end{aligned}
$$

6.7.   The LM test does not depend on the form of the skedastic function. It is not difficult to prove the general case where $\sigma_t^2 = h(z_t'\alpha)$. We start from the log likelihood

$$\ell = -\frac{n}{2}\ln 2\pi - \frac{1}{2}\sum \ln\sigma_t^2 - \frac{1}{2}\sum\frac{u_t^2}{\sigma_t^2}$$

where now $\sigma_t^2 = h(z_t'\alpha)$. The derivatives are

$$s(\alpha) = \frac{\partial\ell}{\partial\alpha} = \frac{1}{2}\sum\frac{h'}{\sigma_t^2}\left(\frac{u_t^2}{\sigma_t^2}-1\right)z_t = \frac{1}{2}\sum\frac{h'}{\sigma_t^2}f_t z_t$$

where $f_t = u_t^2/\sigma_t^2 - 1$ as defined in Appendix 6.1. The block of the information matrix corresponding to α is

$$
\begin{aligned}
I(\alpha) &= -E\left(\frac{\partial\ell}{\partial\alpha\partial\alpha'}\right) \\
&= -E\left(\frac{1}{2}\sum\left[\left(\frac{h''}{\sigma_t^2}-\frac{h'^2}{\sigma_t^4}\right)\left(\frac{u_t^2}{\sigma_t^2}-1\right)-\frac{u_t^2 h'^2}{\sigma_t^6}\right]z_t z_t'\right) \\
&= \frac{1}{2}\sum\frac{h'^2}{\sigma_t^4}z_t z_t'
\end{aligned}
$$

Then

$$s'I^{-1}s = \left(\frac{1}{2}\sum\frac{h'}{\sigma_t^2}f_t z_t\right)'\left(\frac{1}{2}\sum\frac{h'^2}{\sigma_t^4}z_t z_t'\right)^{-1}\left(\frac{1}{2}\sum\frac{h'}{\sigma_t^2}f_t z_t\right)$$

Notice that at this point we cannot pull σ_t^2 nor h' out of the summation sign since it depends on t. But when evaluated at the restricted estimates $\tilde\sigma^2$, they can be treated as a constant and pulled out of the summation sign. Therefore

$$LM = \tilde{s}'\tilde{I}^{-1}\tilde{s} = \frac{1}{2}(\sum\tilde{f}_t z_t)'(\sum z_t z_t')^{-1}(\sum\tilde{f}_t z_t)$$

which is identical to the one given in Appendix 6.1.

6.8.   The R^2 from the original regression is

$$R_y^2 = \frac{b'X'Ay}{y'Ay}$$

where $A = I - ii'/n$ is the deviation-from-mean operator. The transformed dependent variable $z = c_1 y + c_2 i$ has deviation-from-mean of

$$Az = c_1 Ay + c_2 Ai = c_1 Ay$$

so the transformed regression in deviation-from-mean form is $Az = AXb_* + e_*$ where

$$b_* = (X'AX)^{-1}X'Az = (X'AX)^{-1}X'(c_1 Ay) = c_1 b$$

Therefore the R^2 from the transformed dependent variable is

$$R_z^2 = \frac{b_*'X'Az}{z'Az} = \frac{(c_1 b)'X'(c_1 Ay)}{(c_1 Ay)'(c_1 Ay)} = \frac{b'X'Ay}{y'Ay} = R_y^2$$

6.9. The AR(1) process is

$$u_t = \varphi u_{t-1} + \epsilon_t \qquad \text{where} \qquad |\varphi| < 1 \quad \text{and} \quad \epsilon_t \sim iid(0, \sigma_\epsilon^2)$$

To derive the (unconditional) mean of u_t, calculate the successive conditional expectations as

$$\begin{aligned}
E_{t-1}(u_t) &= \varphi u_{t-1} \\
E_{t-2}(u_t) &= E_{t-2}[E_{t-1}(u_t)] = E_{t-2}(\varphi u_{t-1}) = \varphi^2 u_{t-2} \\
&\vdots \\
E_0(u_t) &= \varphi^t u_0
\end{aligned}$$

Then

$$E(u_t) = \lim_{t \to \infty} E_0(u_t) = 0$$

from the stationarity condition $|\varphi| < 1$.

For the second moment, we have

$$u_t^2 = \varphi^2 u_{t-1}^2 + 2\varphi u_{t-1}\epsilon_t + \epsilon_t^2$$

and the successive conditional expectations are

$$\begin{aligned}
E_{t-1}(u_t^2) &= \varphi^2 u_{t-1}^2 + \sigma_\epsilon^2 \\
E_{t-2}(u_t^2) &= E_{t-2}[E_{t-1}(u_t^2)] = E_{t-2}(\varphi^2 u_{t-1}^2 + \sigma_\epsilon^2) = \varphi^4 u_{t-2}^2 + \sigma_\epsilon^2(1 + \varphi^2) \\
&\vdots \\
E_0(u_t^2) &= \varphi^{2t} u_0^2 + \sigma_\epsilon^2(1 + \varphi^2 + \varphi^4 + \cdots + \varphi^{2(t-1)})
\end{aligned}$$

Therefore

$$E(u_t^2) = \lim_{t \to \infty} E_0(u_t^2) = \frac{\sigma_\epsilon^2}{1 - \varphi^2}$$

Chapter 7

7.1. Follow the steps in section 7.1.1 and write the system (P, Q are the endogenous variables, while Y is an exogenous variable) in matrix form as

$$\begin{bmatrix} 1 & -\alpha_1 \\ -(\beta_1 + \beta_2)L + \beta_2 L^2 & 1 \end{bmatrix} \begin{bmatrix} P_t \\ Q_t \end{bmatrix} = \begin{bmatrix} \alpha_0 & \alpha_2 \\ \beta_0 & 0 \end{bmatrix} \begin{bmatrix} D_t \\ Y_t \end{bmatrix} + \begin{bmatrix} u_t \\ v_t \end{bmatrix}$$

$$\begin{aligned} A(L)x_t &= Bz_t + w_t \\ |A(L)|\, x_t &= C(L)Bz_t + C(L)w_t \end{aligned}$$

$$\left(1 - \alpha_1(\beta_1 + \beta_2)L + \alpha_1\beta_2 L^2\right) \begin{bmatrix} P_t \\ Q_t \end{bmatrix} =$$

$$\begin{bmatrix} 1 & \alpha_1 \\ (\beta_1 + \beta_2)L - \beta_2 L^2 & 1 \end{bmatrix} \begin{bmatrix} \alpha_0 & \alpha_2 \\ \beta_0 & 0 \end{bmatrix} \begin{bmatrix} D_t \\ Y_t \end{bmatrix} + \begin{bmatrix} 1 & \alpha_1 \\ (\beta_1 + \beta_2)L - \beta_2 L^2 & 1 \end{bmatrix} \begin{bmatrix} u_t \\ v_t \end{bmatrix}$$

Both equations have the same AR(2) coefficients.

7.2. To obtain the autocorrelation function, first square both sides of the equation and take expectations to get the variance

$$\gamma_0 = E(u_t^2) = (1 + \beta_1^2 + \beta_2^2)\sigma_\epsilon^2$$

Then multiply both sides of the equation by successive lags of itself and take expectations to get the autocovariances

$$\begin{aligned} \gamma_1 &= E(u_t u_{t-1}) &=& -\beta_1(1 - \beta_2)\sigma_\epsilon^2 \\ \gamma_2 &= E(u_t u_{t-2}) &=& -\beta_2 \sigma_\epsilon^2 \\ \gamma_k &= E(u_t u_{t-k}) &=& 0 \qquad \text{for} \quad k = 3, 4, \ldots \end{aligned}$$

Therefore the autocorrelations are

$$\begin{aligned} \rho_0 &= 1, \\ \rho_1 &= \frac{\gamma_1}{\gamma_0} = \frac{-\beta_1(1 - \beta_2)}{1 + \beta_1^2 + \beta_2^2}, \\ \rho_2 &= \frac{\gamma_2}{\gamma_0} = \frac{-\beta_2}{1 + \beta_1^2 + \beta_2^2}, \\ \rho_3 &= \rho_4 = \cdots = 0. \end{aligned}$$

The partial autocorrelations are the coefficients of the AR representation. To obtain the AR representation invert the MA process

$$u_t = (1 - \beta_1 L - \beta_2 L^2)\epsilon_t$$

$$\frac{u_t}{1 - \beta_1 L - \beta_2 L^2} = \epsilon_t$$

$$\frac{1}{\lambda_2 - \lambda_1}\left(\frac{\lambda_2}{1 - \lambda_2 L} - \frac{\lambda_1}{1 - \lambda_1 L}\right) u_t = \epsilon_t$$

$$\frac{1}{\lambda_2 - \lambda_1}\left(\lambda_2(1 + \lambda_2 L + \lambda_2^2 L^2 + \cdots) - \lambda_1(1 + \lambda_1 L + \lambda_1^2 L^2 + \cdots)\right) u_t = \epsilon_t$$

$$\frac{1}{\lambda_2 - \lambda_1}\left(\lambda_2 - \lambda_1 + (\lambda_2^2 - \lambda_1^2)L + \cdots + (\lambda_2^{s+1} - \lambda_1^{s+1})L^s + \cdots\right) u_t = \epsilon_t$$

$$u_t = -(\lambda_2 + \lambda_1)u_{t-1} - \cdots - \frac{\lambda_2^{s+1} - \lambda_1^{s+1}}{\lambda_2 - \lambda_1}u_{t-s} - \cdots + \epsilon_t$$

The sth partial autocorrelation is $-(\lambda_2^{s+1} - \lambda_1^{s+1})/(\lambda_2 - \lambda_1)$, where λ_1, λ_2 are the roots of the characteristic equation $\lambda^2 - \beta_1\lambda - \beta_2 = 0$.

7.3.   ARMA(2,1) model $x_t = a_1 x_{t-1} + a_2 x_{t-2} + \epsilon_t - b\epsilon_{t-1}$.

Square both sides and take expectations (noting that $E[x_{t-1}\epsilon_{t-1}] = \sigma_\epsilon^2$) to get

$$(1 - a_1^2 - a_2^2)\gamma_0 = 2a_1 a_2 \gamma_1 + (1 - 2a_1 b + b^2)\sigma_\epsilon^2 \tag{7.1}$$

Then multiply both sides of x_t by successive lags of itself and take expectations to get

$$(1 - a_2)\gamma_1 = a_1\gamma_0 - b\sigma_\epsilon^2 \tag{7.2}$$
$$\gamma_k = a_1\gamma_{k-1} + a_2\gamma_{k-2} \quad \text{for } k = 2, 3, \ldots$$

Solving (7.1),(7.2) for γ_0, γ_1 yields (after some tedious algebra)

$$\gamma_0 = \frac{1 - a_2 - 2a_1 b + (1 - a_2)b^2}{(1 + a_2)(1 - a_1 - a_2)(1 + a_1 - a_2)}\sigma_\epsilon^2$$

$$\gamma_1 = \frac{a_1 - (1 + a_1^2 - a_2^2)b + a_1 b^2}{(1 + a_2)(1 - a_1 - a_2)(1 + a_1 - a_2)}\sigma_\epsilon^2$$

and the autocorrelations are

$$\rho_0 = 1,$$
$$\rho_1 = \frac{\gamma_1}{\gamma_0} = \frac{a_1 - (1 + a_1^2 - a_2^2)b + a_1 b^2}{1 - a_2 - 2a_1 b + (1 - a_2)b^2},$$
$$\rho_k = \frac{\gamma_k}{\gamma_0} = a_1\rho_{k-1} + a_2\rho_{k-2} \quad \text{for } k = 2, 3, \ldots$$

ARMA(2,2) model $x_t = a_1 x_{t-1} + a_2 x_{t-2} + \epsilon_t - b_1\epsilon_{t-1} - b_2\epsilon_{t-2}$.

Lag the equation once and multiply both sides by ϵ_{t-1} and ϵ_{t-2} to see that

$$E(x_{t-1}\epsilon_{t-1}) = \sigma_\epsilon^2$$
$$E(x_{t-1}\epsilon_{t-2}) = (a_1 - b_1)\sigma_\epsilon^2$$

Square both sides and take expectations to get

$$(1 - a_1^2 - a_2^2)\gamma_0 = 2a_1a_2\gamma_1 + \left(1 - 2a_2b_2 + b_1^2 + b_2^2 - 2a_1b_1(1 - b_2) - 2a_1^2b_2\right)\sigma_\epsilon^2 \qquad (7.3)$$

Multiply both sides of x_t by successive lags of itself and take expectations to get

$$(1 - a_2)\gamma_1 = a_1\gamma_0 - (b_1(1 - b_2) + a_1b_2)\sigma_\epsilon^2 \qquad (7.4)$$
$$\gamma_2 = a_1\gamma_1 + a_2\gamma_0 - b_2\sigma_\epsilon^2 \qquad (7.5)$$
$$\gamma_k = a_1\gamma_{k-1} + a_2\gamma_{k-2} \quad \text{for } k = 3, 4, \ldots$$

The three equations (7.3),(7.4),(7.5) allow us to solve (after some unbelievably tedious algebra) for $\gamma_0, \gamma_1, \gamma_2$. The autocorrelations are then given by

$$\rho_0 = 1,$$
$$\rho_1 = \gamma_1/\gamma_0,$$
$$\rho_2 = \gamma_2/\gamma_0,$$
$$\rho_k = a_1\rho_{k-1} + a_2\rho_{k-2} \quad \text{for } k = 3, 4, \ldots$$

Note that the autocorrelations of ARMA(2,1) and ARMA(2,2) processes follow the same (Yule-Walker) difference equation but with different initial values.

7.4.

$$u_t = \alpha u_{t-1} + \epsilon_t = \epsilon_t + \alpha\epsilon_{t-1} + \alpha^2\epsilon_{t-2} + \cdots$$

Lag once and subtract to get

$$\Delta u_t = \epsilon_t + (\alpha - 1)\epsilon_{t-1} + \alpha(\alpha - 1)\epsilon_{t-2} + \cdots \qquad (7.6)$$

Therefore the mean and variance of Δu_t are

$$E(\Delta u_t) = 0$$

$$\gamma_0 = E[(\Delta u_t)^2] = \left(1 + (\alpha - 1)^2(1 + \alpha^2 + \alpha^4 + \cdots)\right)\sigma_\epsilon^2 = \frac{2\sigma_\epsilon^2}{1 + \alpha}$$

To find the autocovariances of Δu_t note that from (7.6)

$$E(\Delta\epsilon_t\Delta u_{t-1}) = E(\epsilon_t - \epsilon_{t-1})(\epsilon_{t-1} + (\alpha - 1)\epsilon_{t-2} + \cdots) = -\sigma_\epsilon^2$$
$$E(\Delta\epsilon_t\Delta u_{t-2}) = E(\epsilon_t - \epsilon_{t-1})(\epsilon_{t-2} + (\alpha - 1)\epsilon_{t-3} + \cdots) = 0$$

Write Δu_t as $\Delta u_t = \alpha\Delta u_{t-1} + \Delta\epsilon_t$ and multiply both sides by successive lags of Δu_t and take expectations to get

$$\gamma_1 = \alpha\gamma_0 - \sigma_\epsilon^2 = \frac{\alpha - 1}{\alpha + 1}\sigma_\epsilon^2$$
$$\gamma_k = \alpha\gamma_{k-1} = \alpha^{k-1}\gamma_1 \quad \text{for } k = 2, 3, \ldots$$

The autocorrelations are

$$\rho_0 = 1,$$
$$\rho_1 = \frac{\gamma_1}{\gamma_0} = \frac{\alpha - 1}{2},$$
$$\rho_k = \alpha^{k-1}\rho_1 \quad \text{for } k = 2, 3, \ldots$$

7.5. Invert the process to get the AR representation and take the partial derivative.

(a)

$$
\begin{aligned}
u_t &= (1-\alpha L)^{-1}(1-\beta L)\epsilon_t \\
&= (1-\beta L)(1+\alpha L+\alpha^2 L^2+\cdots)\epsilon_t \\
&= \left(1+(\alpha-\beta)L+\alpha(\alpha-\beta)L^2+\cdots+\alpha^{t-s-1}(\alpha-\beta)L^s+\cdots\right)\epsilon_t \\
&= \epsilon_t+(\alpha-\beta)\epsilon_{t-1}+\alpha(\alpha-\beta)\epsilon_{t-2}+\cdots+\alpha^{t-s-1}(\alpha-\beta)\epsilon_{t-s}+\cdots \\
u_{t+s} &= \epsilon_{t+s}+(\alpha-\beta)\epsilon_{t+s-1}+\cdots+\alpha^{t-1}(\alpha-\beta)\epsilon_t+\cdots \\
\frac{\partial u_{t+s}}{\partial \epsilon_t} &= \begin{cases} \alpha^{t-1}(\alpha-\beta) & \text{for} \quad |\alpha|<1 \\ 1-\beta & \text{for} \quad \alpha=1 \end{cases}
\end{aligned}
$$

(b)

$$
\begin{aligned}
u_t &= \frac{1}{(1-L)(1-\alpha L)}\epsilon_t \\
&= \frac{1}{1-\alpha}\left(\frac{1}{1-L}-\frac{\alpha}{1-\alpha L}\right)\epsilon_t \\
&= \frac{1}{1-\alpha}\left(1+L+L^2+\cdots-\alpha(1+\alpha L+\alpha^2 L^2+\cdots)\right)\epsilon_t \\
&= \frac{1}{1-\alpha}\left((1-\alpha)+(1-\alpha^2)L+\cdots+(1-\alpha^{s+1})L^s+\cdots\right)\epsilon_t \\
&= \frac{1}{1-\alpha}\left((1-\alpha)\epsilon_t+(1-\alpha^2)\epsilon_{t-1}+\cdots+(1-\alpha^{s+1})\epsilon_{t-s}+\cdots\right) \\
u_{t+s} &= \epsilon_{t+s}+(1+\alpha)\epsilon_{t+s-1}+\cdots+\frac{1-\alpha^{s+1}}{1-\alpha}\epsilon_t+\cdots \\
\frac{\partial u_{t+s}}{\partial \epsilon_t} &= \frac{1-\alpha^{s+1}}{1-\alpha}
\end{aligned}
$$

7.6.   The ADF test for $Y2$ (with constant and trend and no lagged first differences) yields

```
        Augmented Dickey-Fuller Unit Root Test on Y2
========================================================
ADF Test Statistic  -2.158306     1%   Critical Value*-4.0521
                                  5%   Critical Value -3.4548
                                 10% Critical Value  -3.1528

========================================================
*MacKinnon critical values for rejection of hypothesis of a unit root.
```

```
Augmented Dickey-Fuller Test Equation
LS // Dependent Variable is D(Y2)
Sample: 101 200
Included observations: 100
========================================================
     Variable    CoefficienStd. Errort-Statistic  Prob.
========================================================
      Y2(-1)     -0.093490   0.043316  -2.158306   0.0334
         C        16.48385   7.378390   2.234071   0.0278
```

```
     @TREND(101)       0.165681   0.077651   2.133664   0.0354
==============================================================
R-squared              0.047391   Mean dependent var 1.716788
Adjusted R-squared     0.027750   S.D. dependent var 9.425206
S.E. of regression     9.293512   Akaike info criter 4.488174
Sum squared resid      8377.829   Schwarz criterion  4.566329
Log likelihood        -363.3025   F-statistic        2.412819
Durbin-Watson stat     2.021640   Prob(F-statistic)  0.094920
==============================================================
```

The null hypothesis of a unit root in $Y2$ is not rejected. (Recall that $Y2$ was generated as a random walk with drift.)

The ADF test for $Y5$ (with constant and trend and no lagged first differences) yields

```
        Augmented Dickey-Fuller Unit Root Test on Y5
==============================================================
ADF Test Statistic  -3.720402   1%   Critical Value*-4.0521
                                5%   Critical Value -3.4548
                                10% Critical Value  -3.1528
==============================================================
```
*MacKinnon critical values for rejection of hypothesis of a unit root.

```
Augmented Dickey-Fuller Test Equation
LS // Dependent Variable is D(Y5)
Sample: 101 200
Included observations: 100
==============================================================
     Variable    CoefficienStd. Errort-Statistic  Prob.
==============================================================
        Y5(-1)   -0.199722   0.053683  -3.720402   0.0003
          C       31.56096   8.255139   3.823190   0.0002
     @TREND(101) -0.043990   0.032908  -1.336729   0.1844
==============================================================
R-squared              0.128571   Mean dependent var 0.535557
Adjusted R-squared     0.110603   S.D. dependent var 9.911906
S.E. of regression     9.347705   Akaike info criter 4.499802
Sum squared resid      8475.820   Schwarz criterion  4.577958
Log likelihood        -363.8840   F-statistic        7.155693
Durbin-Watson stat     2.011274   Prob(F-statistic)  0.001263
==============================================================
```

Now the null hypothesis of a unit root is rejected at 5% significance (but not at 1%). Since the trend term is not significant in the test regression, one may run the ADF test without a trend term. The result is

```
        Augmented Dickey-Fuller Unit Root Test on Y5
==============================================================
ADF Test Statistic  -3.524881   1%   Critical Value*-3.4965
                                5%   Critical Value -2.8903
```

10% Critical Value -2.5819
===
*MacKinnon critical values for rejection of hypothesis of a unit root.

Augmented Dickey-Fuller Test Equation
LS // Dependent Variable is D(Y5)
Sample: 101 200
Included observations: 100
===
      Variable   CoefficienStd. Errort-Statistic Prob.
===
        Y5(-1)   -0.186951   0.053038 -3.524881   0.0006
           C   27.53885   7.718043   3.568113   0.0006
===
R-squared   0.112518   Mean dependent var 0.535557
Adjusted R-squared   0.103462   S.D. dependent var 9.911906
S.E. of regression   9.385156   Akaike info criter 4.498056
Sum squared resid   8631.954   Schwarz criterion 4.550159
Log likelihood   -364.7966   F-statistic   12.42478
Durbin-Watson stat   1.999524   Prob(F-statistic) 0.000646
===

With this specification the null hypothesis of a unit root is reject (even at the 1% significance level). Unit root tests may be sensitive to the specification of the test regression (whether you include a constant and/or trend and how many lagged first differences you include).

7.7.

$$A(L)(y_t - \delta_0 - \delta_1 t) = \epsilon_t$$
$$(1 - \alpha_1 L - \alpha_2 L^2)(y_t - \delta_0 - \delta_1 t) = \epsilon_t$$

$$y_t = -\delta_0(1 + \alpha_1 + \alpha_2) + \delta_1(\alpha_1 + 2\alpha_2) + \delta_1(1 - \alpha_1 - \alpha_2)t + \alpha_1 y_{t-1} + \alpha_2 y_{t-2} + \epsilon_t$$

This is the estimated equation. Comparing the coefficients with the fitted regression, we get

$$\alpha_1 = 1.335, \quad \alpha_2 = -0.401, \quad \delta_0 = 1.749, \quad \delta_1 = 0.0455$$

For $A(L) = 1 - 1.335L + 0.401L^2$, we have

$$\begin{aligned} A(1) &= 1 - 1.335 + 0.401 = 0.066 > 0 \\ A(2) &= 1 - 2.670 + 1.604 = -0.066 < 0 \\ A(3) &= 1 - 4.005 + 3.609 = 0.604 > 0 \end{aligned}$$

The two roots both lie outside the unit circle and the estimated autoregressive part satisfies the stationarity condition. (Recall that when there is a unit root $A(1) = 0$.) The first regression suggests that y_t is trend stationary.

We can rewrite the second equation as

$$\begin{aligned} y_t - y_{t-1} &= 0.003 + 0.369(y_{t-1} - y_{t-2}) + \nu_t \\ y_t &= 0.003 + 1.369 y_{t-1} - 0.369 y_{t-2} + \nu_t \end{aligned}$$

This is an AR(2) without a deterministic trend. For the lag polynomial $B(L) = 1 - 1.369L + 0.369L^2$, we have

$$\begin{array}{rcccrcl}
B(1) & = & 1 - 1.369 + 0.369 & = & 0 & & \\
B(2) & = & 1 - 2.738 + 1.476 & = & -0.262 & < & 0 \\
B(3) & = & 1 - 4.107 + 3.321 & = & 0.214 & > & 0
\end{array}$$

We now have one unit root and one root outside the unit circle. The second regression suggests that y_t is difference stationary.

7.8. By repeated substitution, we have

$$\begin{aligned}
y_{n+s} - \mu & = & \alpha(y_{n+s-1} - \mu) + \epsilon_{n+s} - \beta\epsilon_{n+s-1} \\
& = & \alpha\left(\alpha(y_{n+s-2} - \mu) + \epsilon_{n+s-1} - \beta\epsilon_{n+s-2}\right) + \epsilon_{n+s} - \beta\epsilon_{n+s-1} \\
& \vdots & \\
& = & \alpha^s(y_n - \mu) + \epsilon_{n+s} + (\alpha - \beta)\epsilon_{n+s-1} + \cdots + \alpha^{s-2}(\alpha - \beta)\epsilon_{n+1} - \alpha^{s-1}\beta\epsilon_n
\end{aligned}$$

Therefore

$$\widehat{y}_{n+s} - \mu = E(y_{n+s} - \mu | I_n) = \alpha^s(y_n - \mu) - \alpha^{s-1}\beta\epsilon_n$$

and

$$e_{n+s} = y_{n+s} - \widehat{y}_{n+s} = \epsilon_{n+s} + (\alpha - \beta)\epsilon_{n+s-1} + \cdots + \alpha^{s-2}(\alpha - \beta)\epsilon_{n+1}$$

$$E(e_{n+s}^2) = \sigma_\epsilon^2 \left(1 + (\alpha - \beta)^2 + \cdots + \alpha^{2(s-2)}(\alpha - \beta)^2\right) \to \sigma_\epsilon^2 \left(\frac{1 - 2\alpha\beta + \beta^2}{1 - \alpha^2}\right) \quad \text{as } s \to \infty$$

7.9.

$$z_{n+s} = z_n + y_{n+1} + \cdots + y_{n+s} = (z_n + s\mu) + (y_{n+1} - \mu) + \cdots + (y_{n+s} - \mu)$$

The terms $y_{n+k} - \mu$ $(k = 1, 2, \cdots, s)$ can be written as

$$y_{n+k} - \mu = \alpha^k(y_n - \mu) + \epsilon_{n+k} + \alpha\epsilon_{n+k-1} + \cdots + \alpha^{k-1}\epsilon_{n+1}$$

Then

$$\begin{aligned}
z_{n+s} & = & z + s\mu + \alpha(1 + \alpha + \cdots + \alpha^{s-1})(y_n - \mu) \\
& & + (1 + \alpha + \cdots + \alpha^{s-1})\epsilon_{n+1} + (1 + \alpha + \cdots + \alpha^{s-2})\epsilon_{n+2} + \cdots + \epsilon_{n+s} \\
& = & z + s\mu + \frac{\alpha(1 - \alpha^s)}{1 - \alpha}(y_n - \mu) + e_{n+s}
\end{aligned}$$

and

$$E(e_{n+s}^2) = \sigma_\epsilon^2 \left((1 + \alpha + \cdots + \alpha^{s-1})^2 + (1 + \alpha + \cdots + \alpha^{s-2})^2 + \cdots + (1 + \alpha)^2 + 1\right)$$

7.10. To fit an ARMA model to the seasonal difference $\Delta_{12} HS_t = HS_t - HS_{t-12}$, we first look at the correlogram of $\Delta_{12} HS_t$

```
                   Correlogram of D(HS,0,12)
===============================================================
Sample: 1959:01 1984:12
Included observations: 300
===============================================================
 Autocorrelation Partial Correlation  AC      PAC  Q-Stat  Prob
```

```
================================================================
     .|*******|        .|*******|    1  0.869 0.869  228.56 0.000
     .|****** |        .|**    |    2  0.818 0.261  432.18 0.000
     .|****** |        .|.     |    3  0.756 0.017  606.44 0.000
     .|*****  |        .|.     |    4  0.690-0.050  752.09 0.000
     .|*****  |        *|.     |    5  0.618-0.076  869.40 0.000
     .|****   |        *|.     |    6  0.546-0.063  961.42 0.000
     .|****   |        *|.     |    7  0.472-0.065 1030.3 0.000
     .|***    |        .|.     |    8  0.401-0.042 1080.2 0.000
     .|***    |        .|.     |    9  0.338-0.008 1115.8 0.000
     .|**     |        *|.     |   10  0.253-0.122 1135.7 0.000
     .|*      |        .|.     |   11  0.189-0.022 1146.9 0.000
     .|*      |       **|.     |   12  0.080-0.221 1148.9 0.000
     .|*      |        .|***   |   13  0.087 0.340 1151.3 0.000
     .|.      |        .|.     |   14  0.040-0.009 1151.8 0.000
     .|.      |        *|.     |   15 -0.009-0.102 1151.9 0.000
     .|.      |        *|.     |   16 -0.057-0.106 1152.9 0.000
     *|.      |        .|*     |   17 -0.077 0.067 1154.8 0.000
     *|.      |        *|.     |   18 -0.116-0.071 1159.2 0.000
     *|.      |        *|.     |   19 -0.160-0.110 1167.4 0.000
    **|.      |        .|.     |   20 -0.190-0.019 1179.1 0.000
    **|.      |        *|.     |   21 -0.242-0.095 1198.1 0.000
    **|.      |        .|.     |   22 -0.260-0.023 1220.1 0.000
    **|.      |        .|.     |   23 -0.288 0.004 1247.2 0.000
    **|.      |        *|.     |   24 -0.301-0.061 1276.9 0.000
   ***|.      |        .|*     |   25 -0.330 0.108 1312.7 0.000
   ***|.      |        .|.     |   26 -0.326 0.031 1347.9 0.000
   ***|.      |        *|.     |   27 -0.336-0.083 1385.3 0.000
   ***|.      |       **|.     |   28 -0.364-0.218 1429.3 0.000
   ***|.      |        .|.     |   29 -0.395-0.031 1481.4 0.000
   ***|.      |        .|.     |   30 -0.411-0.042 1538.0 0.000
   ***|.      |        *|.     |   31 -0.419-0.060 1597.1 0.000
   ***|.      |        .|.     |   32 -0.438-0.048 1661.9 0.000
   ***|.      |        .|.     |   33 -0.436-0.022 1726.3 0.000
   ***|.      |        .|.     |   34 -0.441 0.007 1792.7 0.000
   ***|.      |        .|.     |   35 -0.431 0.021 1856.3 0.000
   ***|.      |        *|.     |   36 -0.445-0.148 1924.4 0.000
================================================================
```

There are still some spikes at lags 1, 12, and 13 so we still fit a mixed seasonal ARMA model to $\Delta_{12}HS_t$.

```
============================================================
LS // Dependent Variable is D(HS,0,12)
Sample(adjusted): 1961:02 1984:12
Included observations: 287 after adjusting endpoints
Convergence achieved after 31 iterations
============================================================
     Variable     CoefficienStd. Errort-Statistic  Prob.
```

```
================================================================
      C          1.523769   2.025559   0.752271   0.4525
    AR(1)        0.949658   0.020334  46.70341    0.0000
   SAR(12)       0.106312   0.058223   1.825948   0.0689
    MA(1)       -0.193965   0.058771  -3.300366   0.0011
   SMA(12)      -0.885825   0.000135 -6581.558    0.0000
================================================================
R-squared             0.859879   Mean dependent var 1.787108
Adjusted R-squared    0.857892   S.D. dependent var 32.58395
S.E. of regression   12.28326    Akaike info criter 5.033743
Sum squared resid   42547.74     Schwarz criterion  5.097497
Log likelihood      -1124.577    F-statistic        432.6367
Durbin-Watson stat    2.026645   Prob(F-statistic)  0.000000
================================================================
```

The correlogram of $y_t = (1 - L)(1 - L^{12})HS_t$ is

```
                   Correlogram of Y
================================================================
Sample: 1959:01 1984:12
Included observations: 299
================================================================
Autocorrelation Partial Correlation  AC    PAC  Q-Stat Prob
================================================================
   **|.      |      **|.     |  1-0.310-0.310 29.027 0.000
    .|.      |       *|.     |  2 0.044-0.058 29.609 0.000
    .|.      |        .|.    |  3 0.014 0.012 29.673 0.000
    .|.      |        .|.    |  4 0.020 0.034 29.795 0.000
    .|.      |        .|.    |  5 0.002 0.022 29.797 0.000
    .|.      |        .|.    |  6 0.011 0.020 29.835 0.000
    .|.      |        .|.    |  7-0.011-0.004 29.873 0.000
    .|.      |        .|.    |  8-0.030-0.040 30.149 0.000
    .|*      |        .|*    |  9 0.084 0.068 32.337 0.000
    *|.      |        .|.    | 10-0.078-0.034 34.208 0.000
    .|*      |        .|*    | 11 0.165 0.149 42.747 0.000
  ***|.      |     ***|.     | 12-0.437-0.394 102.52 0.000
    .|**     |        .|.    | 13 0.205-0.030 115.78 0.000
    .|.      |        .|*    | 14 0.015 0.066 115.85 0.000
    .|.      |        .|.    | 15-0.007 0.058 115.87 0.000
    *|.      |       *|.     | 16-0.105-0.113 119.38 0.000
    .|*      |        .|.    | 17 0.078 0.028 121.30 0.000
    .|.      |        .|.    | 18 0.017 0.062 121.40 0.000
    .|.      |        .|.    | 19-0.053-0.038 122.31 0.000
    .|*      |        .|.    | 20 0.083 0.033 124.52 0.000
    *|.      |        .|.    | 21-0.130-0.043 129.95 0.000
    .|.      |       *|.     | 22 0.037-0.067 130.39 0.000
    .|.      |        .|.    | 23-0.057-0.007 131.44 0.000
    .|.      |       *|.     | 24 0.057-0.167 132.48 0.000
    *|.      |       *|.     | 25-0.122-0.078 137.34 0.000
```

```
 .|.          |       .|.         | 26  0.047 0.044 138.07 0.000
 .|*          |       .|*         | 27  0.074 0.163 139.90 0.000
 .|.          |       .|.         | 28  0.009-0.035 139.93 0.000
 *|.          |       .|.         | 29-0.059-0.033 141.10 0.000
 .|.          |       .|.         | 30-0.034-0.013 141.49 0.000
 .|.          |       .|.         | 31  0.044-0.028 142.14 0.000
 *|.          |       *|.         | 32-0.088-0.066 144.74 0.000
 .|.          |       *|.         | 33  0.033-0.083 145.11 0.000
 .|.          |       *|.         | 34-0.057-0.084 146.22 0.000
 .|*          |       .|*         | 35  0.089 0.079 148.89 0.000
 *|.          |      **|.         | 36-0.177-0.237 159.56 0.000
================================================================
```

There are still some spikes at lags 1, 12, and 13 so we still fit a mixed seasonal ARMA model to y_t.

```
================================================================
LS // Dependent Variable is D(HS,1,12)
Sample(adjusted): 1961:03 1984:12
Included observations: 286 after adjusting endpoints
Convergence achieved after 20 iterations
================================================================
       Variable    CoefficienStd. Errort-Statistic  Prob.
================================================================
            C     -0.024352  0.101674  -0.239510   0.8109
          AR(1)   -0.065289  0.252622  -0.258445   0.7963
        SAR(12)    0.096642  0.057249   1.688102   0.0925
          MA(1)   -0.150952  0.254897  -0.592207   0.5542
        SMA(12)   -0.885359  0.000135 -6539.255    0.0000
================================================================
R-squared            0.440843  Mean dependent var 0.025175
Adjusted R-squared   0.432883  S.D. dependent var 16.50153
S.E. of regression  12.42683   Akaike info criter 5.057044
Sum squared resid   43393.75   Schwarz criterion  5.120960
Log likelihood      -1123.974  F-statistic        55.38549
Durbin-Watson stat   2.050881  Prob(F-statistic)  0.000000
================================================================
```

(Students should check whether the residuals from each model are nearly white noise.) One way to compare these two models with the mixed seasonal ARMA model estimated in Table 7.17 is to compare the forecasts from the three models. The forecasts from the mixed seasonal ARMA model fitted in Table 7.17 ($HSF1$), fitted to $\Delta_{12} HS_t$ ($HSF2$), and fitted to $y_t = (1 - L)(1 - L^{12}) HS_t$ ($HSF3$) are summarized below. (The forecast period is 85.01–92.04 for 88 observations.)

	$HSF1$	$HSF2$	$HSF3$
Root Mean Squared Error	28.44461	35.19723	19.75908
Mean Absolute Error	23.00396	27.97521	15.84251
Mean Absolute Percentage Error	22.86921	28.26311	14.76571
Theil Inequality Coefficient	0.109212	0.131043	0.078792

The last model for $y_t = (1 - L)(1 - L^{12})HS_t$ has the best forecasting performance.

Chapter 8

8.1. The residuals from Eq. (A8.4) can be written as $e_4 = M y_t$ where $M = I - X(X'X)^{-1}X'$ is the residual maker matrix and $X = [y_{t-1} \;\; x_t]$. Since Eq. (A8.5) has the same right-hand side variables as Eq. (A8.4), the residuals from Eq. (A8.5) are

$$e_5 = M\Delta y_t = My_t - My_{t-1}.$$

The second term My_{t-1} is the residual from regressing y_{t-1} on X and is identically equal to zero since X contains the regressand y_{t-1}.

8.2. Write y_t and y_{t-1} in terms of first differences and y_{t-2} as

$$
\begin{aligned}
y_{t-1} &= y_{t-2} + \Delta y_{t-1} \\
y_t &= y_{t-2} + \Delta y_{t-1} + \Delta y_t
\end{aligned}
$$

and similary for x_t and x_{t-1}. Substitute into Eq. (8.12) to get

$$
\begin{aligned}
y_{t-2} + \Delta y_{t-1} + \Delta y_t =\ & m + \alpha_1(y_{t-2} + \Delta y_{t-1}) + \alpha_2 y_{t-2} \\
& + \beta_0(x_{t-2} + \Delta x_{t-1} + \Delta x_t) + \beta_1(x_{t-2} + \Delta x_{t-1}) \\
& + \beta_2 x_{t-2} + \epsilon_t \\
\Delta y_t =\ & m - (1-\alpha_1)\Delta y_{t-1} + \beta_0 \Delta x_t + (\beta_0 + \beta_1)\Delta x_{t-1} \\
& - (1 - \alpha_1 - \alpha_2)y_{t-2} + (\beta_0 + \beta_1 + \beta_2)x_{t-2} + \epsilon_t \\
\Delta y_t =\ & m - (1-\alpha_1)\Delta y_{t-1} + \beta_0 \Delta x_t + (\beta_0 + \beta_1)\Delta x_{t-1} \\
& - (1 - \alpha_1 - \alpha_2)(y_{t-2} - \gamma x_{t-2}) + \epsilon_t
\end{aligned}
$$

8.3. For a unit elasticity specification $\gamma = 1$. Substituting into Eq. (8.13) gives

$$\Delta y_t = m - \alpha_2 \Delta y_{t-1} + \beta_0 \Delta x_t - \beta_2 \Delta x_{t-1} - (1 - \alpha_1 - \alpha_2)(y_{t-1} - x_{t-1}) + \epsilon_t$$

This can be estimated by regressing Δy_t on a constant, Δy_{t-1}, Δx_t, Δx_{t-1}, and $(y_{t-1} - x_{t-1})$. Alternatively, we can use the reparameterization derived in Problem 8.2 above. Substituting $\gamma = 1$ yields

$$\Delta y_t = m - (1-\alpha_1)\Delta y_{t-1} + \beta_0 \Delta x_t + (\beta_0 + \beta_1)\Delta x_{t-1} - (1 - \alpha_1 - \alpha_2)(y_{t-2} - x_{t-2}) + \epsilon_t$$

This is a regression of Δy_t on a constant, Δy_{t-1}, Δx_t, Δx_{t-1}, and $(y_{t-2} - x_{t-2})$. The two regressions will yield identical residuals.

8.4.   From the Frisch-Waugh-Lovell Theorem (see Appendix 3.2) the residuals from regressing y on x and z is identical to the residuals from regressing $M_x y$ on $M_x z$ where $M_x = I_n - x(x'x)^{-1}x'$. Therefore the esitmated residuals from Eq. (8.16) can be written as

$$e = M M_x y \quad \text{where} \quad M = I_n - M_x z(z'M_x z)^{-1} z' M_x.$$

Since the "true" model is $y = x\beta + u$, we have

$$e = M M_x(x\beta + u) = M M_x u$$

and the estimated residual variance is

$$s^2 = \frac{e'e}{n-2} = \frac{u'M_x M M_x u}{n-2}$$

Using the usual trick of taking the expectation of the trace, we have

$$
\begin{aligned}
E(s^2) &= E\left[\mathrm{tr}(u'M_x M M_x u)\right]/(n-2) \\
&= E\left[\mathrm{tr}(M_x M M_x uu')\right]/(n-2) \\
&= \mathrm{tr}\left(M_x M M_x E[uu']\right)/(n-2) \\
&= \mathrm{tr}(\sigma^2 M_x M M_x)/(n-2) \\
&= \sigma^2 \mathrm{tr}(M_x M M_x)/(n-2)
\end{aligned}
$$

By the definition of M

$$
\begin{aligned}
M_x M M_x &= M_x[I_n - M_x z(z'M_x z)^{-1} z' M_x]M_x \\
&= M_x - M_x z(z'M_x z)^{-1} z' M_x \\
&= M_x + M - I_n
\end{aligned}
$$

and

$$\mathrm{tr}(M_x) = \mathrm{tr}\left(I_n - x(x'x)^{-1}x'\right) = n - 1$$
$$\mathrm{tr}(M) = \mathrm{tr}\left(I_n - M_x z(z'M_x z)^{-1} z' M_x\right) = n - 1$$

Therefore

$$
\begin{aligned}
E(s^2) &= \sigma^2 \mathrm{tr}(M_x M M_x)/(n-2) \\
&= \sigma^2 \mathrm{tr}(M_x + M - I_n)/(n-2) \\
&= \sigma^2 \left(\mathrm{tr}(M_x) + \mathrm{tr}(M) - \mathrm{tr}(I_n)\right)/(n-2) \\
&= \sigma^2(n - 1 + n - 1 - n)/(n-2) \\
&= \sigma^2
\end{aligned}
$$

8.5.   **Omitted variables.** The specification is

$$y = X_1 \beta_1 + u$$

whereas the "true" model is

$$y = X_1 \beta_1 + X_2 \beta_2 + v$$

The OLS estimate of β_1 is

$$
\begin{aligned}
b_1 &= (X_1'X_1)^{-1}X_1'y \\
&= (X_1'X_1)^{-1}X_1'(X_1\beta_1 + X_2\beta_2 + v) \\
&= \beta_1 + (X_1'X_1)^{-1}X_1'X_2\beta_2 + (X_1'X_1)^{-1}X_1'v
\end{aligned}
$$

Assuming $E(v|X_1) = 0$, we have

$$
\begin{aligned}
E(b_1) &= \beta_1 + (X_1'X_1)^{-1}X_1'X_2\beta_2 \\
E(b_1) - \beta_1 &= (X_1'X_1)^{-1}X_1'X_2\beta_2
\end{aligned}
$$

The OLS estimate of β_1 is biased unless $X_1'X_2 = 0$.

Irrelevant variables. The specification is.

$$
y = X_1\beta_1 + X_2\beta_2 + v
$$

whereas the true model is

$$
y = X_1\beta_1 + u
$$

The OLS estimates of β_1 and β_2 are

$$
\begin{aligned}
b_1 &= (X_1'M_2X_1)^{-1}X_1'M_2y \\
&= (X_1'M_2X_1)^{-1}X_1'M_2(X_1\beta_1 + u) \\
&= \beta_1 + (X_1'M_2X_1)^{-1}X_1'M_2u \\
b_2 &= (X_2'M_1X_2)^{-1}X_2'M_1y \\
&= (X_2'M_1X_2)^{-1}X_2'M_1(X_1\beta_1 + u) \\
&= (X_2'M_1X_2)^{-1}X_2'M_1u
\end{aligned}
$$

where the last equality follows from $M_1X_1 = 0$. Assuming that u is uncorrelated with X_1 and X_2, we have

$$
E(b_1) = \beta_1 \qquad \text{and} \qquad E(b_2) = 0
$$

8.6.   We first show that the two regressions

$$
\begin{aligned}
e_y &= xb_1 + e_xb_2 + \widehat{u} \\
y &= x\widehat{\beta}_1 + e_x\widehat{\beta}_2 + \widehat{v}
\end{aligned}
$$

yield the same estimated coefficient on e_x ($b_2 = \widehat{\beta}_2$) and the same residuals ($\widehat{u} = \widehat{v}$). Premultiply both sides of the first regression by $M_1 = I - x(x'x)^{-1}x'$ and use $M_1x = 0$ to get

$$
M_1e_y = M_1e_xb_2 + M_1\widehat{u} = M_1e_xb_2 + \widehat{u}
$$

where the second line follows from $x'\widehat{u} = 0$. From the Frisch-Waugh Theorem and noting that $e_y = M_1y$ we have

$$
b_2 = (e_x'M_1e_x)^{-1}e_x'M_1e_y = (e_x'M_1e_x)^{-1}e_x'M_1y
$$

$$
\widehat{u} = NM_1e_y = NM_1y
$$

where $N = I - M_1e_x(e_x'M_1e_x)^{-1}e_x'M_1$.

Similary, for the second regression, premultiply both sides by M_1 to get

$$M_1 y = M_1 e_x \widehat{\beta}_2 + M_1 \widehat{v} = M_1 e_x \widehat{\beta}_2 + \widehat{v}$$

From the Frisch-Waugh Theorem

$$\widehat{\beta}_2 = (e_x' M_1 e_x)^{-1} e_x' M_1 y$$
$$\widehat{v} = N M_1 y$$

This shows the first part $b_2 = \widehat{\beta}_2$ and $\widehat{u} = \widehat{v}$.

We next show the relation between the F-statistic for testing $b_2 = 0$ and the nR^2 from the first regression. The F-statistic is

$$F = \frac{(RRSS - URSS)/r}{URSS/(n-k)} = \frac{(e_y' M_1 e_y - \widehat{u}'\widehat{u})/r}{\widehat{u}'\widehat{u}/(n-k)} = \frac{(y' M_1 y - \widehat{u}'\widehat{u})/r}{\widehat{u}'\widehat{u}/(n-k)}$$

where the last equality follows from $e_y = M_1 y$. The R^2 from the first regression is

$$R^2 = \frac{ESS}{TSS} = \frac{TSS - RSS}{TSS} = \frac{e_y' e_y - \widehat{u}'\widehat{u}}{e_y' e_y} = \frac{y' M_1 y - \widehat{u}'\widehat{u}}{y' M_1 y}$$

Therefore we have

$$rF = \frac{y' M_1 y - \widehat{u}'\widehat{u}}{\widehat{u}'\widehat{u}/(n-k)}$$
$$nR^2 = \frac{y' M_1 y - \widehat{u}'\widehat{u}}{y' M_1 y/n}$$

Under the null hypothesis of $b_2 = 0$, both $URSS/(n-k) = \widehat{u}'\widehat{u}/(n-k)$ and $RRSS/n = y' M_1 y/n$ are consistent estimates of σ^2. Therefore both rF and nR^2 are asymptotically distributed as $\chi^2(r)$ under the null hypothesis.

8.7.   Using the identity

$$y_{t-1} = \Delta y_{t-1} + y_{t-2} \quad \text{and} \quad y_t = \Delta y_t + \Delta y_{t-1} + y_{t-2} \quad .$$

we can reparameterize the ADL(2,2) as

$$\begin{aligned}
\Delta y_t + \Delta y_{t-1} + y_{t-2} &= m + \alpha_1(\Delta y_{t-1} + y_{t-2}) + \alpha_2 y_{t-2} \\
&\quad + \beta_0(\Delta x_t + \Delta x_{t-1} + x_{t-2}) \\
&\quad + \beta_1(\Delta x_{t-1} + x_{t-2}) + \beta_2 x_{t-2} + \epsilon \\
\Delta y_t &= m - (1 - \alpha_1)\Delta y_{t-1} - (1 - \alpha_1 - \alpha_2)y_{t-2} + \beta_0 \Delta x_t \\
&\quad + (\beta_0 + \beta_1)\Delta x_{t-1} + (\beta_0 + \beta_1 + \beta_2)x_{t-2} + \epsilon
\end{aligned}$$

Assuming that y, x are mean-zero difference stationary, we find that α_1, β_0, and β_1 are coefficients of mean-zero I(0) variables. Alternatively, if we use the identity $y_{t-2} = y_{t-1} - \Delta y_{t-1}$ we have the reparameterization

$$\Delta y_t = m - \alpha_2 \Delta y_{t-1} - (1 - \alpha_1 - \alpha_2)y_{t-1} + \beta_0 \Delta x_t + (\beta_0 + \beta_1)\Delta x_{t-1} + (\beta_0 + \beta_1 + \beta_2)x_{t-2} + \epsilon$$

and $\alpha_2, \beta_0, \beta_1$ are coefficients of mean-zero I(0) variables. If we use the identity $x_{t-2} = x_{t-1} - \Delta x_{t-1}$ the reparameterization is

$$\Delta y_t = m - (1 - \alpha_1)\Delta y_{t-1} - (1 - \alpha_1 - \alpha_2)y_{t-2} + \beta_0 \Delta x_t - \beta_2 \Delta x_{t-1} + (\beta_0 + \beta_1 + \beta_2)x_{t-1} + \epsilon$$

and $\alpha_1, \beta_0, \beta_2$ are coefficients of mean-zero I(0) variables. Not all of $\beta_0, \beta_1, \beta_2$ can be written as coefficients of mean-zero I(0) variables.

8.8. Perron (1989) develops three tests of a unit root assuming a one-time change in (A) the level of the linear trend, (B) the slope of the linear trend, and (C) both the level and slope of the linear trend. Here I illustrate how to carry out test (C) for the expenditure (Y) and price ($X2$) series used in Section 8.4. (Figure 8.1 indicates possibly two structural changes, in which case Perron's test is not applicable.) As a preliminary step, we need to generate three series

$$DU_t = \begin{cases} 1 & \text{if } t > T_B \\ 0 & \text{otherwise} \end{cases}$$

$$DT_t = \begin{cases} t & \text{if } t > T_B \\ 0 & \text{otherwise} \end{cases}$$

$$D(TB)_t = \begin{cases} 1 & \text{if } t = T_B + 1 \\ 0 & \text{otherwise} \end{cases}$$

where T_B is the time of the one-time shift. The test is then carried out by estimating

$$\Delta y_t = c_0 + c_1 DU_t + c_2 t + c_3 DT_t + c_4 D(TB)_t + b_0 y_{t-1} + b_1 \Delta y_{t-1} + \cdots + b_k \Delta y_{t-k}$$

and referring the t-statistic on y_{t-1} to the critical values tabulated in Perron (1989). I chose $T_B = 73.3$, $k = 3$ so that $\lambda = T_B/T = 0.46$. (The critical values depend on λ.)

```
===========================================================
LS // Dependent Variable is D(Y)
Sample(adjusted): 1960:1 1990:4
Included observations: 124 after adjusting endpoints
===========================================================
    Variable    CoefficienStd. Errort-Statistic  Prob.
===========================================================
        C       -1.330007   0.443866  -2.996417   0.0033
        DU       0.054517   0.027250   2.000603   0.0478
        t        0.001427   0.000464   3.076834   0.0026
        DT      -0.001392   0.000498  -2.795237   0.0061
        D_TB     0.007162   0.018985   0.377244   0.7067
        Y(-1)   -0.165079   0.054800  -3.012396   0.0032
        D(Y(-1))-0.082676   0.094196  -0.877708   0.3819
        D(Y(-2))-0.125191   0.092606  -1.351862   0.1791
        D(Y(-3))-0.056677   0.093018  -0.609309   0.5435
===========================================================
R-squared          0.172364   Mean dependent var 0.002383
Adjusted R-squared 0.114790   S.D. dependent var 0.019004
S.E. of regression 0.017880   Akaike info criter-7.978377
Sum squared resid  0.036763   Schwarz criterion -7.773679
Log likelihood     327.7110   F-statistic        2.993750
Durbin-Watson stat 1.956553   Prob(F-statistic)  0.004372
===========================================================


===========================================================
LS // Dependent Variable is D(X2)
Sample(adjusted): 1960:1 1990:4
Included observations: 124 after adjusting endpoints
===========================================================
    Variable    CoefficienStd. Errort-Statistic  Prob.
===========================================================
        C        0.341019   0.123699   2.756851   0.0068
        DU       0.025436   0.026922   0.944798   0.3467
        t       -0.000198   0.000335  -0.591277   0.5555
        DT       3.94E-05   0.000406   0.096932   0.9229
        D_TB     0.035786   0.040213   0.889922   0.3754
```

X2(-1)	-0.072716	0.025997	-2.797040	0.0060
D(X2(-1))	0.436443	0.091917	4.748216	0.0000
D(X2(-2))	-0.090362	0.100131	-0.902436	0.3687
D(X2(-3))	0.130550	0.095070	1.373195	0.1724

R-squared	0.233416	Mean dependent var	0.000864
Adjusted R-squared	0.180088	S.D. dependent var	0.042102
S.E. of regression	0.038123	Akaike info criter	-6.464084
Sum squared resid	0.167133	Schwarz criterion	-6.259386
Log likelihood	233.8248	F-statistic	4.377024
Durbin-Watson stat	1.931054	Prob(F-statistic)	0.000122

The 5% critical values are -4.22 ($\lambda = 0.4$) and -4.24 ($\lambda = 0.5$); neither series reject the null hypothesis of a unit root (even at 10%).

8.9.   Expanding the second line of Eq. (8.54) gives

$$(\beta_0 + \beta_1 + \beta_2 + \beta_3 + \beta_4 + \beta_5)L + \delta_0 + \delta_1 L + \delta_2 L^2 \delta_3 L^3 + \delta_4 L^4 - \delta_0 L - \delta_1 L^2 - \delta_2 L^3 - \delta_3 L^4 - \delta_4 L^5 =$$
$$\delta_0 + (\beta_0 + \beta_1 + \beta_2 + \beta_3 + \beta_4 + \beta_5 + \delta_1 - \delta_0)L + (\delta_2 - \delta_1)L^2 + (\delta_3 - \delta_2)L^3 + (\delta_4 - \delta_3)L^4 - \delta_4 L^5$$

Comparing this with the first line of Eq. (8.54), we must have

$$\begin{cases} \beta_0 = \delta_0 \\ \beta_1 = \beta_0 + \beta_1 + \beta_2 + \beta_3 + \beta_4 + \beta_5 + \delta_1 - \delta_0 \\ \beta_2 = \delta_2 - \delta_1 \\ \beta_3 = \delta_3 - \delta_2 \\ \beta_4 = \delta_4 - \delta_3 \\ \beta_5 = -\delta_4 \end{cases} \quad \text{or} \quad \begin{cases} \delta_0 = \beta_0 \\ \delta_1 = -(\beta_2 + \beta_3 + \beta_4 + \beta_5) \\ \delta_2 = -(\beta_3 + \beta_4 + \beta_5) \\ \delta_3 = -(\beta_4 + \beta_5) \\ \delta_4 = -\beta_5 \end{cases}$$

8.10.   An example is provided by Table 8.7 (in levels) and Table 8.8 (in first differences). The two regressions have identical residuals and all diagnostic statistics based on the residuals are identical: s.e. of regression, sum of squared residuals, log likelihood (see Eq. 5.7), DW test (see Eq. 6.42), and the information criteria (which are based on the log likelihood and the number of parameters). The R^2 (adjusted and unadjusted) and F-statistics differ between the two specifications since they depend on the left-hand side variable. (The restricted RSS in the F-statistic is the sum of squares of the left-hand side variable.)

8.11.   The static and dynamic forecasts are summarized below.

	Static	Dynamic
Root Mean Squared Error	0.016752	0.017602
Mean Absolute Error	0.012717	0.013137
Mean Absolute Percentage Error	0.165536	0.171180
Theil Inequality Coefficient	0.001090	0.001145

In general, static forecasts perform better than dynamic forecasts; forecast errors accumulate in dynamic forecasts.

Chapter 9

9.1. The following program in EViews generates a two variable VAR(1) with

$$A = \begin{bmatrix} 0.4 & 0.2 \\ 0.6 & 0.1 \end{bmatrix}$$

$$E(uu') = \begin{bmatrix} 1 & 0.5 \\ 0.5 & 3 \end{bmatrix}$$

Note that this A matrix has two eigenvalues with moduli less than one (Case 1 of the Section 9.1).

```
create u 200 'create workfile

scalar n=200 'set n=obs

scalar a11=0.4 'assign A matrix
scalar a12=0.2
scalar a21=0.6
scalar a22=0.1

scalar m1=0 'assign constant m vector
scalar m2=0

sym(2) cov 'declare covariance matrix of errors
sym cov(1,1)=1 'assign covariance
sym cov(2,1)=0.5
sym cov(2,2)=4

rndseed 123456789 'set seed of random number

matrix(n,2) u 'declare matrix to fill errors
nrnd(u) 'fill u with iid std normal
u=@transpose(@cholesky(cov)*@transpose(u)) 'tansform u to have covariance=cov
mtos(u,dog) 'convert u into two series ser1 ser2

smpl 1 1 'set initial values of y
genr y1=0
genr y2=0

for !i=2 to n 'recuresively genr y
smpl !i !i
```

```
genr y1=m1+a11*y1(-1)+a12*y2(-1)+ser1
genr y2=m2+a21*y1(-1)+a22*y2(-1)+ser2
next
```

```
smpl @all
```

Let the students apply the unit root tests and cointegration tests to the generated series.

9.2.   The eigenvalues of A are given by solving the characteristic equation

$$|A - \lambda I| = -(\lambda - 1)^2(\lambda - \frac{1}{2}) = 0$$

which yields $\lambda = 1, 1, 0.5$; A has two unit roots and a single stationary root. Since rank Π = rank $(I - A) = 2$, there should be two cointegrating relations. The case when

$$A = \begin{bmatrix} 1 & 0 & 0 \\ 0 & 1 & 0 \\ 1 & 1 & 0.5 \end{bmatrix}$$

is explained in the text where $a = 0.5$. In this case rank $\Pi = 1$ and there should be a single cointegrating relation.

9.3.   When the disturbances are pairwise uncorrelated, $\sigma_{ij} = 0$ for $i \neq j$. Then

$$\Sigma^{-1} = \begin{bmatrix} \frac{1}{\sigma_1} I_n & & 0 \\ & \ddots & \\ 0 & & \frac{1}{\sigma_m} I_n \end{bmatrix}$$

and

$$X'\Sigma^{-1}X = \begin{bmatrix} X_1' & & 0 \\ & \ddots & \\ 0 & & X_m' \end{bmatrix} \begin{bmatrix} \frac{1}{\sigma_1}I & & 0 \\ & \ddots & \\ 0 & & \frac{1}{\sigma_m}I \end{bmatrix} \begin{bmatrix} X_1 & & 0 \\ & \ddots & \\ 0 & & X_m \end{bmatrix}$$

$$= \begin{bmatrix} \frac{1}{\sigma_1}X_1'X_1 & & 0 \\ & \ddots & \\ 0 & & \frac{1}{\sigma_m}X_m'X_m \end{bmatrix}$$

$$X'\Sigma^{-1}y = \begin{bmatrix} \frac{1}{\sigma_1}X_1'y_1 \\ \vdots \\ \frac{1}{\sigma_m}X_m'y_m \end{bmatrix}$$

The SUR estimator is then

$$b_{GLS} = (X'\Sigma^{-1}X)^{-1}X'\Sigma^{-1}y$$

$$= \begin{bmatrix} \sigma_1(X_1'X_1)^{-1} & & 0 \\ & \ddots & \\ 0 & & \sigma_m(X_m'X_m)^{-1} \end{bmatrix} \begin{bmatrix} \frac{1}{\sigma_1}X_1'y_1 \\ \vdots \\ \frac{1}{\sigma_m}X_m'y_m \end{bmatrix}$$

$$= \begin{bmatrix} (X_1'X_1)^{-1}X_1'y_1 \\ \vdots \\ (X_m'X_m)^{-1}X_m'y_m \end{bmatrix}$$

which is OLS applied to each equation separately.

When the matrix of explanatory variables is the same in each equation, $X_1 = X_2 = \cdots = X_m$. Then we can write

$$X = \begin{bmatrix} X_1 & & 0 \\ & \ddots & \\ 0 & & X_m \end{bmatrix} = I_m \otimes X_k$$

for any k and[1]

$$
\begin{aligned}
X'\Sigma^{-1}X &= (I \otimes X_k)'(\Sigma_c^{-1} \otimes I)(I \otimes X_k) \\
&= (I \otimes X_k')(\Sigma_c^{-1} \otimes I)(I \otimes X_k) \\
&= \Sigma_c^{-1} \otimes X_k'X_k \\
X'\Sigma^{-1}y &= (I \otimes X_k')(\Sigma_c^{-1} \otimes I)y \\
&= (\Sigma_c^{-1} \otimes X_k')y
\end{aligned}
$$

The SUR estimator is then

$$
\begin{aligned}
b_{GLS} &= (X'\Sigma^{-1}X)^{-1}X'\Sigma^{-1}y \\
&= (\Sigma_c^{-1} \otimes X_k'X_k)^{-1}(\Sigma_c^{-1} \otimes X_k')y \\
&= \left(\Sigma_c \otimes (X_k'X_k)^{-1}\right)\left(\Sigma_c^{-1} \otimes X_k'\right)y \\
&= \left(I_m \otimes (X_k'X_k)^{-1}X_k'\right)y \\
&= \begin{bmatrix} (X_1'X_1)^{-1}X_1' & & 0 \\ & \ddots & \\ 0 & & (X_m'X_m)^{-1}X_m' \end{bmatrix} \begin{bmatrix} y_1 \\ \vdots \\ y_m \end{bmatrix} \\
&= \begin{bmatrix} (X_1'X_1)^{-1}X_1'y_1 \\ \vdots \\ (X_m'X_m)^{-1}X_m'y_m \end{bmatrix}
\end{aligned}
$$

which is again OLS applied to each equation separately.

9.4. First normalize the innovation to the second variable as

$$u_2 = \epsilon_2/s_2$$

and let

$$u_1 = (\epsilon_1 - b_{12}\epsilon_2)/s_{1.2}$$

where

$$s_2 = 5, \qquad b_{12} = \frac{cov(\epsilon_1, \epsilon_2)}{var(\epsilon_2)} = 0.56, \qquad s_{1.2} = \sqrt{s_1^2(1 - r_{12}^2)} = 2.8566$$

---

[1] I use the fact that

$$
\begin{aligned}
(A \otimes B)^{-1} &= A^{-1} \otimes B^{-1} \\
(A \otimes B)' &= A' \otimes B' \\
(A \otimes B)(C \otimes D) &= AC \otimes BD
\end{aligned}
$$

Solving for ϵ we get

$$\epsilon_2 = s_2 u_2$$
$$\epsilon_1 = s_{1.2} u_1 + s_2 b_{12} u_2$$

or

$$\epsilon = \begin{bmatrix} s_{1.2} & s_2 b_{12} \\ 0 & s_2 \end{bmatrix} \begin{bmatrix} u_1 \\ u_2 \end{bmatrix}$$
$$= \begin{bmatrix} 2.8566 & 2.8 \\ 0 & 5 \end{bmatrix} \begin{bmatrix} u_1 \\ u_2 \end{bmatrix}$$
$$= P^{-1} u$$

A one standard deviation impulse in the first orthogonal disturbance corresponds to

$$\epsilon_1 = P^{-1} \begin{bmatrix} 1 \\ 0 \end{bmatrix} = \begin{bmatrix} 2.8566 \\ 0 \end{bmatrix}$$

and the response in y can be found from

$$y_1 = \epsilon_1, \quad y_2 = Ay_1 = A\epsilon_1, \quad y_3 = Ay_2 = A^2 \epsilon_1, \quad \cdots$$

Period	y_1	y_2
1	2.8566	0
2	1.1426	0.5713
3	0.5142	0.5142
4	0.2571	0.3599

Compared to Table 9.3, the effect looks much smaller. Similarly, the effect of a one standard deviation impulse in the second orthogonal disturbance can be computed.

Ordering: ϵ_1, ϵ_2

Period	y_1	y_2
1	0	3.5707
2	0.3571	1.7853
3	0.3214	0.9641
4	0.2250	0.5463

Ordering: ϵ_2, ϵ_1

Period	y_1	y_2
1	2.8000	5.0000
2	1.6200	3.0600
3	0.9540	1.8540
4	0.5670	1.1178

9.5. Collect all the variables except the error term on the left-hand side and write the matrix of structural coefficients as

	Y	C	I	W_P	Π	K
C	0	1	0	$-\alpha_1$	$-\alpha_2$	0
I	0	0	1	0	$-\beta_1$	0
W_P	$-\gamma_1$	0	0	1	0	0
Y	1	-1	-1	0	0	0
Π	-1	0	0	1	1	0
K	0	0	-1	0	0	1

	1	G	W_G	T	t	Π_{-1}	K_{-1}	Y_{-1}	T_{-1}	$(W_G)_{-1}$
	$-\alpha_0$	0	$-\alpha_1$	0	0	$-\alpha_3$	0	0	0	0
	$-\beta_0$	0	0	0	0	$-\beta_2$	$-\beta_3$	0	0	0
	$-\gamma_0$	0	γ_1	$-\gamma_1$	$-\gamma_3$	0	0	$-\gamma_2$	$-\gamma_2$	γ_2
	0	-1	0	0	0	0	0	0	0	0
	0	0	0	1	0	0	0	0	0	0
	0	0	0	0	0	0	-1	0	0	0

Checking the order condition, there are 10 variables excluded from the first row. Since $G - 1 = 5$, the consumption function is overidentified. To check the rank condition we look at the columns corresponding to the variables excluded from the first row.

$$
\begin{aligned}
rank(A\Phi) \\
= \ rank &\begin{bmatrix}
0 & 0 & 0 & 0 & 0 & 0 & 0 & 0 & 0 & 0 \\
0 & 1 & 0 & 0 & 0 & 0 & -\beta_3 & 0 & 0 & 0 \\
-\gamma_1 & 0 & 0 & 0 & -\gamma_1 & -\gamma_3 & 0 & -\gamma_3 & -\gamma_3 & -\gamma_3 \\
1 & -1 & 0 & -1 & 0 & 0 & 0 & 0 & 0 & 0 \\
-1 & 0 & 0 & 0 & 1 & 0 & 0 & 0 & 0 & 0 \\
0 & -1 & 1 & 0 & 0 & 0 & -1 & 0 & 0 & 0
\end{bmatrix} \\
= \ 5
\end{aligned}
$$

and the rank condition for identifiability is satisfied.

9.6. There are two endogenous and three exogenous variables in the system. Applying the order condition to the first equation we find that it is overidentified. To find the 2SLS estimates we apply the formula in Eq. (9.60). For this problem

$$
y = y_1, \quad Y_1 = y_2, \quad X_1 = x_1, \quad X_2 = [x_2 \ x_3]
$$

and

$$
Y_1'X = [2\ 1\ 0], \quad Y_1'X_1 = 2, \quad X_1'X_1 = 1, \quad X'y = \begin{bmatrix} 2 \\ 3 \\ 0 \end{bmatrix}, \quad X_1'y = 2
$$

$$
Y_1'X(X'X)^{-1}X'Y_1 = [2\ 1\ 0] \begin{bmatrix} 1 & 0 & 0 \\ 0 & 1 & 0 \\ 0 & 0 & 1 \end{bmatrix}^{-1} \begin{bmatrix} 2 \\ 1 \\ 0 \end{bmatrix} = 5
$$

$$
Y_1'X(X'X)^{-1}X'y = [2\ 1\ 0] \begin{bmatrix} 1 & 0 & 0 \\ 0 & 1 & 0 \\ 0 & 0 & 1 \end{bmatrix}^{-1} \begin{bmatrix} 2 \\ 3 \\ 0 \end{bmatrix} = 7
$$

Substituting into Eq. (9.60) gives the 2SLS estimates as (be careful about the sign)

$$
\begin{bmatrix} \widehat{\beta}_{12} \\ \widehat{\gamma}_{11} \end{bmatrix} = - \begin{bmatrix} 5 & 2 \\ 2 & 1 \end{bmatrix}^{-1} \begin{bmatrix} 7 \\ 2 \end{bmatrix} = \begin{bmatrix} -3 \\ 4 \end{bmatrix}
$$

9.7.

(a) Write the matrix of structural coefficients for each model as

	c	i	y	r	m_{-1}
c	1	0	$-\alpha_1$	0	$-\alpha_2$
i	0	1	$-\beta_1$	$-\beta_2$	0
y	-1	-1	1	0	0

	m	r	m_{-1}	y
m	1	$-\gamma_1$	$-\gamma_2$	0
r	$-\delta_1$	1	$-\delta_2$	$-\delta_3$

We see that all equations are just identified, except for the second equation of model 2; since there are no excluded variables, the second equation (for r_t) in model 2 is not identified.

(b) To find the reduced form, solve each endogenous variable as a function of exogenous variables. For model 1 substitute the last equation (an identity) into the first two equations and get the reduced form of c and i

$$c = \frac{1}{1-\alpha_1-\beta_1}(\alpha_1\beta_2 r + \alpha_2(1-\beta_1)m_{-1} + (1-\beta_1)u_1 + \alpha_1 u_2)$$

$$i = \frac{1}{1-\alpha_1-\beta_1}(\beta_2(1-\alpha_1)r + \alpha_2\beta_1 m_{-1} + \beta_1 u_1 + (1-\alpha_1)u_2)$$

Then

$$y = c + i = \frac{1}{1-\alpha_1-\beta_1}(\beta_2 r + \alpha_2 m_{-1} + u_1 + u_2)$$

For model 2, substitute the first equation into the second and solve for r to get

$$r = \frac{1}{1-\delta_1\gamma_1}((\delta_1\gamma_2 + \delta_2)m_{-1} + \delta_3 y + \delta_1 v_1 + v_2)$$

(c) Write the two reduced form equations as

$$y = a_1 r + a_2 m_{-1} + \epsilon_1$$
$$r = b_1 m_{-1} + b_2 y + \epsilon_2$$

If we regard this as a system with two endogenous variables (y, r) and one exogenous or predetermined variable (m_{-1}), then there are no exclusions in either equations; both equations are not identified.

9.8.

(a) Write the matrix of structural coefficients as

	y_1	y_2	y_3	y_4	y_5	z_1	z_2	z_3	z_4
y_1	1	β_{12}	0	β_{14}	0	γ_{11}	0	0	γ_{14}
y_2	0	1	β_{23}	0	β_{25}	0	γ_{22}	0	0
y_3	0	0	1	0	0	γ_{31}	0	γ_{33}	0
y_4	β_{41}	0	β_{43}	1	0	0	γ_{42}	0	γ_{44}
y_5	0	0	2	0	1	0	-1	0	0

There are 5 endogenous variables and 4 exogenous variables. For an equation to be identified there must be at least 4 exclusion restrictions. According to the order condition, the first and fourth equations are just identified and others are overidentified.

(b) Since the third equation is already overidentified, the conclusion does not change if we add more exclusion restrictions.

(c) For the just identified equations, ILS, 2SLS, and 3SLS all yield identical estimates. For the other overidentified equations, 2SLS or 3SLS give consistent estimates.

9.9. According to the order condition, the first equation is just identified and the second is overidentified.

(a) The unrestricted reduced form parameters are given by

$$\hat{\Pi} = (Z'Z)^{-1}Z'y = \begin{bmatrix} 1 & 0 & 0 \\ 0 & 1 & 1 \\ 0 & 1 & 2 \end{bmatrix}^{-1} \begin{bmatrix} 1 & 1 \\ 1 & 3 \\ 0 & 4 \end{bmatrix} = \begin{bmatrix} 1 & 1 \\ 2 & 2 \\ -1 & 1 \end{bmatrix}$$

(b) Since the first equation is just identified, ILS is identical to 2SLS. To apply the formula in Eq. (9.60), note that

$$y = y_1, \quad Y_1 = y_2, \quad X_1 = [z_1 \; z_2], \quad X_2 = z_3$$

and

$$Y_1'X = [1 \; 3 \; 4], \quad Y_1'X_1 = [1 \; 3], \quad X_1'X_1 = \begin{bmatrix} 1 & 0 \\ 0 & 1 \end{bmatrix}, \quad X'y = \begin{bmatrix} 1 \\ 1 \\ 0 \end{bmatrix}, \quad X_1'y = \begin{bmatrix} 1 \\ 1 \end{bmatrix}$$

$$Y_1'X(X'X)^{-1}X'Y_1 = [1 \; 3 \; 4] \begin{bmatrix} 1 & 0 & 0 \\ 0 & 1 & 1 \\ 0 & 1 & 2 \end{bmatrix}^{-1} \begin{bmatrix} 1 \\ 3 \\ 4 \end{bmatrix} = 11$$

$$Y_1'X(X'X)^{-1}X'y = [1 \; 3 \; 4] \begin{bmatrix} 1 & 0 & 0 \\ 0 & 1 & 1 \\ 0 & 1 & 2 \end{bmatrix}^{-1} \begin{bmatrix} 1 \\ 1 \\ 0 \end{bmatrix} = 3$$

Substituting into Eq. (9.60) gives the 2SLS or ILS estimates

$$\begin{bmatrix} \hat{\beta}_{12} \\ \hat{\gamma}_{11} \\ \hat{\gamma}_{12} \end{bmatrix} = \begin{bmatrix} 11 & 1 & 3 \\ 1 & 1 & 0 \\ 3 & 0 & 1 \end{bmatrix}^{-1} \begin{bmatrix} 3 \\ 1 \\ 1 \end{bmatrix} = \begin{bmatrix} -1 \\ 2 \\ 4 \end{bmatrix}$$

(c) For the second equation we have

$$y = y_2, \quad Y_1 = y_1, \quad X_1 = z_3, \quad X_2 = [z_1 \; z_2]$$

and

$$Y_1'X = [0 \; 1 \; 1], \quad Y_1'X_1 = 0, \quad X_1'X_1 = 2, \quad X'y = \begin{bmatrix} 4 \\ 1 \\ 3 \end{bmatrix}, \quad X_1'y = 4$$

$$Y_1'X(X'X)^{-1}X'Y_1 = [0\ 1\ 1]\begin{bmatrix} 2 & 0 & 1 \\ 0 & 1 & 0 \\ 1 & 0 & 1 \end{bmatrix}^{-1}\begin{bmatrix} 0 \\ 1 \\ 1 \end{bmatrix} = 3$$

$$Y_1'X(X'X)^{-1}X'y = [0\ 1\ 1]\begin{bmatrix} 2 & 0 & 1 \\ 0 & 1 & 0 \\ 1 & 0 & 1 \end{bmatrix}^{-1}\begin{bmatrix} 4 \\ 1 \\ 3 \end{bmatrix} = 3$$

Substituting into Eq. (9.60) gives the 2SLS estimates as

$$\begin{bmatrix} \widehat{\beta}_{21} \\ \widehat{\gamma}_{23} \end{bmatrix} = \begin{bmatrix} 3 & 0 \\ 0 & 2 \end{bmatrix}^{-1}\begin{bmatrix} 3 \\ 4 \end{bmatrix} = \begin{bmatrix} 1 \\ 2 \end{bmatrix}$$

(*d*) The restricted reduced form is

$$y_1 = \frac{1}{1 - \beta_{12}\beta_{21}}(\gamma_{11}z_1 + \gamma_{12}z_2 + \beta_{12}\gamma_{23}z_3 + \epsilon_1 + \beta_{12}\epsilon_2)$$

$$y_2 = \frac{1}{1 - \beta_{12}\beta_{21}}(\beta_{21}\gamma_{11}z_1 + \beta_{21}\gamma_{12}z_2 + \gamma_{23}z_3 + \beta_{21}\epsilon_1 + \epsilon_2)$$

and so the restricted reduced form coefficients are

$$\begin{aligned}
\widetilde{\Pi} &= \frac{1}{1 - \beta_{12}\beta_{21}}\begin{bmatrix} \gamma_{11} & \gamma_{12} & \beta_{12}\gamma_{23} \\ \beta_{21}\gamma_{11} & \beta_{21}\gamma_{12} & \gamma_{23} \end{bmatrix} \\
&= \frac{1}{2}\begin{bmatrix} 2 & 4 & -2 \\ 2 & 4 & 2 \end{bmatrix} \\
&= \begin{bmatrix} 1 & 2 & -1 \\ 1 & 2 & 1 \end{bmatrix}
\end{aligned}$$

The unrestricted and restricted reduced form coefficients happen to be the same! This is, of course, not true in general.

(*e*) (*b*) and (*c*) yield consistent estimates of ϵ as

$$\begin{aligned}
\widehat{\epsilon}_1 &= y_1 + y_2 - 2z_1 - 4z_2 \\
\widehat{\epsilon}_2 &= y_2 - y_1 - 2z_3
\end{aligned}$$

and so a consistent estimate of σ_{12} is

$$\begin{aligned}
\widehat{\sigma}_{12} &= \widehat{\epsilon}_1'\widehat{\epsilon}_2/n \\
&= (y_1 + y_2 - 2z_1 - 4z_2)'(y_2 - y_1 - 2z_3)/n \\
&= -1/n
\end{aligned}$$

where n is the number of observations (not given).

9.10. The first equation is overidentified by the order condition. To apply the 2SLS formula in Eq. (9.60) note that

$$y = y_1, \quad Y_1 = y_2, \quad X_1 = [x_2\ x_3], \quad X_2 = [x_1\ x_4]$$

and

$$Y_1'X = [1.5 \ \ 0.5 \ \ -0.5 \ \ -1], \quad Y_1'X_1 = [1.5 \ \ 0.5],$$

$$X_1'X_1 = \begin{bmatrix} 2 & 0 \\ 0 & 1 \end{bmatrix}, \quad X'y = \begin{bmatrix} 1 \\ -3 \\ 2 \\ -5 \end{bmatrix}, \quad X_1'y = \begin{bmatrix} 1 \\ -3 \end{bmatrix}$$

$$Y_1'X(X'X)^{-1}X'Y_1 = [1.5 \ \ 0.5 \ \ -0.5 \ \ -1] \begin{bmatrix} 3 & 0 & 0 & 0 \\ 0 & 2 & 0 & 0 \\ 0 & 0 & 1 & 0 \\ 0 & 0 & 0 & 0.5 \end{bmatrix}^{-1} \begin{bmatrix} 1.5 \\ 0.5 \\ -0.5 \\ -1 \end{bmatrix} = 3.125$$

$$Y_1'X(X'X)^{-1}X'y = [1.5 \ \ 0.5 \ \ -0.5 \ \ -1] \begin{bmatrix} 3 & 0 & 0 & 0 \\ 0 & 2 & 0 & 0 \\ 0 & 0 & 1 & 0 \\ 0 & 0 & 0 & 0.5 \end{bmatrix}^{-1} \begin{bmatrix} 1 \\ -3 \\ 2 \\ -5 \end{bmatrix} = 8.75$$

Substituting into Eq. (9.60) gives the 2SLS estimates as (be careful about the sign)

$$\begin{bmatrix} \widehat{\beta}_{12} \\ \widehat{\gamma}_{12} \\ \widehat{\gamma}_{13} \end{bmatrix} = - \begin{bmatrix} 3.125 & 1.5 & 0.5 \\ 1.5 & 2 & 0 \\ 0.5 & 0 & 1 \end{bmatrix}^{-1} \begin{bmatrix} 8.75 \\ 1 \\ -3 \end{bmatrix} = \begin{bmatrix} -5.4286 \\ 3.5714 \\ 5.7143 \end{bmatrix}$$

The standard errors are given in Eq. (9.59).

$$
\begin{aligned}
s^2 &= \frac{1}{n}(y - Z_1 a_1)'(y - Z_1 a_1) \\
&= \frac{1}{n}(y'y - 2y'Z_1 a_1 + a_1' Z_1' Z_1 a_1) \\
&= \frac{1}{n}\left(y'y - 2[y'Y_1 \ \ y'X_1]a_1 + a_1' \begin{bmatrix} Y_1'Y_1 & Y_1'X_1 \\ X_1'Y_1 & X_1'X_1 \end{bmatrix} a_1 \right) \\
&= \frac{1}{100}\left(80 - 2[-4 \ 1 \ -3] \begin{bmatrix} -5.4286 \\ 3.5714 \\ 5.7143 \end{bmatrix} \right. \\
&\quad \left. + [-5.4286 \ 3.5714 \ 5.7143] \begin{bmatrix} 5 & 1.5 & 0.5 \\ 1.5 & 2 & 0 \\ 0.5 & 0 & 1 \end{bmatrix} \begin{bmatrix} -5.4286 \\ 3.5714 \\ 5.7143 \end{bmatrix} \right) \\
&= 1.8
\end{aligned}
$$

and so

$$var(a_1) = 1.8 \begin{bmatrix} 3.125 & 1.5 & 0.5 \\ 1.5 & 2 & 0 \\ 0.5 & 0 & 1 \end{bmatrix}^{-1} = \begin{bmatrix} 1.0286 & -0.7714 & -0.5143 \\ & 1.4786 & 0.3857 \\ & & 2.0571 \end{bmatrix}$$

9.11.   The structural equation to be estimated can be written as

$$y_1 = a_1 y_2 + a_2 x_1 + u_1$$

where in the notation of Eq. (9.60)

$$y = y_1, \quad Y_1 = y_2, \quad X_1 = x_1, \quad X_2 = [x_2 \ x_3 \ x_4]$$

Note that this equation is overidentified. The reduced form coefficients of the two endogenous variables are given by $\Pi = (X'X)^{-1}X'Y$ so that we can recover $X'Y$, $Y_1'X(X'X)^{-1}X'Y$ as

$$X'Y = X'X\Pi = \begin{bmatrix} 7 & 0 & 3 & 1 \\ 0 & 2 & -2 & 0 \\ 3 & -2 & 5 & 1 \\ 1 & 0 & 1 & 1 \end{bmatrix} \begin{bmatrix} 0 & 1 \\ 1 & -1 \\ 3 & 1 \\ 2 & -1 \end{bmatrix} = \begin{bmatrix} 11 & 9 \\ -4 & -4 \\ 15 & 9 \\ 5 & 1 \end{bmatrix}$$

$$Y_1'X(X'X)^{-1}X'Y = Y_1'X\Pi = \begin{bmatrix} 9 & -4 & 9 & 1 \end{bmatrix} \begin{bmatrix} 0 & 1 \\ 1 & -1 \\ 3 & 1 \\ 2 & -1 \end{bmatrix} = \begin{bmatrix} 25 & 21 \end{bmatrix}$$

Substituting into Eq. (9.60) gives the 2SLS estimates

$$\begin{bmatrix} a_1 \\ a_2 \end{bmatrix} = \begin{bmatrix} 21 & 9 \\ 9 & 7 \end{bmatrix}^{-1} \begin{bmatrix} 25 \\ 11 \end{bmatrix} = \begin{bmatrix} 1.51 \\ 0.09 \end{bmatrix}$$

9.12.   The first equation is overidentified. From the information of the variance of the reduced form for y_1 we have

$$var(\Pi_1) = s^2(X'X)^{-1} = 2(X'X)^{-1} = \begin{bmatrix} 1 & 0 & 0 \\ 0 & 0.5 & 0 \\ 0 & 0 & 0.1 \end{bmatrix}$$

and so

$$(X'X)^{-1} = \begin{bmatrix} 0.5 & 0 & 0 \\ 0 & 0.25 & 0 \\ 0 & 0 & 0.05 \end{bmatrix}$$

$$X'X = \begin{bmatrix} 2 & 0 & 0 \\ 0 & 4 & 0 \\ 0 & 0 & 20 \end{bmatrix}$$

From the reduced form coefficients we have

$$\Pi = (X'X)^{-1}X'[y \ Y_1]$$
$$[X'y \ X'Y_1] = (X'X)\Pi$$
$$= \begin{bmatrix} 2 & 0 & 0 \\ 0 & 4 & 0 \\ 0 & 0 & 20 \end{bmatrix} \begin{bmatrix} 5 & 10 \\ 10 & 10 \\ 2 & 5 \end{bmatrix}$$
$$= \begin{bmatrix} 10 & 20 \\ 40 & 40 \\ 40 & 100 \end{bmatrix}$$

and

$$Y_1'X(X'X)^{-1}X'Y_1 = [20\ 40\ 100] \begin{bmatrix} 10 \\ 10 \\ 5 \end{bmatrix} = 1100$$

$$Y_1'X(X'X)^{-1}X'y = [20\ 40\ 100] \begin{bmatrix} 5 \\ 10 \\ 2 \end{bmatrix} = 700$$

Substituting into Eq. (9.60) gives the 2SLS estimates

$$\begin{bmatrix} \widehat{\beta}_{12} \\ \widehat{\gamma}_{11} \end{bmatrix} = \begin{bmatrix} 1100 & 20 \\ 20 & 2 \end{bmatrix}^{-1} \begin{bmatrix} 700 \\ 10 \end{bmatrix} = \begin{bmatrix} 0.6667 \\ -1.6667 \end{bmatrix}$$

9.13. The equation is overidentified. In the notation of Eq. (9.60)

$$y = y_1, \quad Y_1 = [y_2 \ \ y_3], \quad X_1 = x_1, \quad X_2 = [x_2\ x_3\ x_4]$$

and

$$Y_1'X = \begin{bmatrix} 0 & 4 & 12 & -5 \\ 0 & -2 & -12 & 10 \end{bmatrix},$$

$$Y_1'X_1 = \begin{bmatrix} 0 \\ 0 \end{bmatrix}, \quad X_1'X_1 = 1, \quad X'y = \begin{bmatrix} 2 \\ 2 \\ 4 \\ 5 \end{bmatrix}, \quad X_1'y = 2,$$

$$Y_1'X(X'X)^{-1}X'Y_1 = \begin{bmatrix} 49 & -50 \\ -50 & 58 \end{bmatrix}, \quad Y_1'X(X'X)^{-1}X'y = \begin{bmatrix} 11 \\ -4 \end{bmatrix}$$

Substituting into Eq. (9.60) gives the 2SLS estimates

$$\begin{bmatrix} \widehat{\beta}_{12} \\ \widehat{\beta}_{13} \\ \widehat{\gamma}_{11} \end{bmatrix} = \begin{bmatrix} 49 & -50 & 0 \\ -50 & 58 & 0 \\ 0 & 0 & 1 \end{bmatrix}^{-1} \begin{bmatrix} 11 \\ -4 \\ 2 \end{bmatrix} = \begin{bmatrix} 1.2807 \\ 1.0351 \\ 2.000 \end{bmatrix}$$

The standard errors are given in Eq. (9.59).

$$\begin{aligned} s^2 &= \frac{1}{n}(y - Z_1 a_1)'(y - Z_1 a_1) \\ &= \frac{1}{n}(y'y - 2y'Z_1 a_1 + a_1' Z_1' Z_1 a_1 \\ &= \frac{1}{n}\left(y'y - 2[y'Y_1 \ y'X_1]a_1 + a_1' \begin{bmatrix} Y_1'Y_1 & Y_1'X_1 \\ X_1'Y_1 & X_1'X_1 \end{bmatrix} a_1 \right) \\ &= \frac{1}{30}\left(20 - 2[15 \ -5 \ 2] \begin{bmatrix} 1.2807 \\ 1.0351 \\ 2.000 \end{bmatrix} \right. \\ &\qquad \left. +[1.2807\ 1.0351\ 2.000] \begin{bmatrix} 60 & -45 & 0 \\ -45 & 70 & 0 \\ 0 & 0 & 1 \end{bmatrix} \begin{bmatrix} 1.2807 \\ 1.0351 \\ 2.000 \end{bmatrix} \right) \\ &= 1.4011 \end{aligned}$$

and so

$$var(a_1) = 1.4011 \begin{bmatrix} 49 & -50 & 0 \\ -50 & 58 & 0 \\ 0 & 0 & 1 \end{bmatrix}^{-1} = \begin{bmatrix} 0.2376 & 0.2048 & 0 \\ & 0.2007 & 0 \\ & & 1.4011 \end{bmatrix}$$

Chapter 10

10.1. The density function $f(x)$ is shown below.

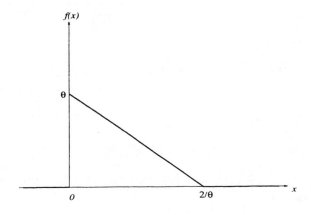

(a) To show that $f(x)$ is a density, we need to show

$$f(x) \geq 0 \quad \text{for all } x \qquad \text{and} \qquad \int f(x)dx = 1.$$

Looking at the graph, the former is obvious and the latter requires the area under $f(x)$ to be 1; the triangle area is $\theta \times 2/\theta \times 1/2 = 1$.

(b)

$$E(X) = \int_0^{\frac{2}{\theta}} x f(x)dx = \int_0^{\frac{2}{\theta}} x \left(\theta - \frac{\theta^2}{2}x \right) dx = \frac{2}{3\theta}$$

(c) Matching the sample mean with the population mean found in (b), we have the moment condition

$$\frac{\sum x_i}{n} = \frac{2}{3\theta}.$$

Solving for θ yields the method of moments estimator

$$\widehat{\theta} = \frac{2n}{3\sum x_i}.$$

One can also match higher moments with a little more algebra; it is also more tedious to calculate the corresponding variance.

10.2.   For those who received the treatment, the regression equation is

$$y^t = \alpha + \beta.$$

This is just a regression of y^t on a constant, which gives the mean effect among the treatment group:

$$\widehat{\alpha} + \widehat{\beta} = \overline{y}^t$$

For those who received the placebo, the regression equation is

$$y^c = \alpha$$

and the constant is the mean effect among the control group:

$$\widehat{\alpha} = \overline{y}^c$$

Solving for $\widehat{\alpha}$, $\widehat{\beta}$ yields

$$\widehat{\alpha} = \overline{y}^c, \qquad \widehat{\beta} = \overline{y}^t - \overline{y}^c$$

10.3.   We need to show that

$$(G'WG)^{-1}G'W\Omega WG(G'WG)^{-1} - (G'\Omega^{-1}G)^{-1}$$
$$= (G'WG)^{-1}G'W\left[\Omega - G(G'\Omega^{-1}G)^{-1}G'\right]WG(G'WG)^{-1}$$

is positive semi-definite. This follows if the expression in square brackets

$$\Psi = \Omega - G(G'\Omega^{-1}G)^{-1}G'$$

is positive semi-definite. Since Ω is positive definite, we can write $\Omega = \phi'\phi$, where ϕ is a positive definite symmetric matrix. Then

$$
\begin{aligned}
\Psi &= \phi'\phi - G\left[G'\phi^{-1}(\phi')^{-1}G\right]^{-1}G' \\
&= \phi'\left\{I - (\phi')^{-1}G\left[G'\phi^{-1}(\phi')^{-1}G\right]^{-1}G'\phi^{-1}\right\}\phi \\
&= \phi'M\phi
\end{aligned}
$$

where the expression in curly brackets M is symmetric idempotent. This shows that Ψ is positive semi-definite.

10.4.   The GMM estimator under heteroskedasticity is given in Eq. (10.39) as

$$\hat{\beta}_{GMM} = \left[X'Z(\widehat{Z'\Omega Z})^{-1}Z'X\right]^{-1}X'Z(\widehat{Z'\Omega Z})^{-1}Z'y.$$

When 2SLS is exactly identified, Z and X have the same column rank and $Z'X$ is an invertible square matrix. Thus Eq. (10.39) simplifies to

$$
\begin{aligned}
\hat{\beta}_{GMM} &= (Z'X)^{-1}\widehat{Z'\Omega Z}(X'Z)^{-1}X'Z(\widehat{Z'\Omega Z})^{-1}Z'y \\
&= (Z'X)^{-1}Z'y
\end{aligned}
$$

which is the 2SLS estimator for the exactly identified case.

10.5. Since the restricted *RSS* from both equations are obtained by regressing y on X and are the same, we only need to show that the unrestricted *RSS* from the two equations are the same as well; that is, we need to show that the residuals from the two equations are the same. To see this, rewrite Eq. (10.55) as

$$
\begin{aligned}
y &= X\beta + \hat{x}_1\delta \\
&= X\beta + P_Z x_1\delta \\
&= x_1\beta_1 + x_2\beta_2 + (I - M_Z)x_1\delta \\
&= x_1(\beta_1 + \delta) + x_2\beta_2 - M_Z x_1\delta
\end{aligned}
$$

The last line is a regression of y on $X = [x_1 \quad x_2]$ and the residuals from regressing x_1 on Z $(M_Z x_1)$. The two regressions give identical residuals.

10.6. The moment condition to be tested is

$$
\frac{1}{n}e'Z = 0
$$

where e is the OLS residual from regressing c_{t+1} on a constant and c_t. The minimized quadratic form is

$$
\begin{aligned}
&\frac{1}{n^2}e'Z\left(var\left(\frac{1}{n}e'Z\right)\right)^{-1}Z'e \\
=\ &\frac{1}{n^2}e'Z\left(\frac{s^2}{n^2}Z'Z\right)^{-1}Z'e \\
=\ &\frac{e'Z(Z'Z)^{-1}Z'e}{s^2} \\
=\ &\frac{e'e - e'M_Z e}{e'e/N}
\end{aligned}
$$

where the second term in the numerator $e'M_Z e$ is the *RSS* from regressing e on Z. This *RSS* is identical to the *RSS* from regressing e on y_t alone since e is orthogonal to the other elements of Z (constant and c_t) by construction.

10.7.

(a) Using the identity $g = w + h$, we can rewrite the regression as

$$
\begin{aligned}
\Delta h &= \eta\Delta w + \text{error} \\
&= \eta(\Delta g - \Delta h) + \text{error} \\
(1+\eta)\Delta h &= \eta\Delta g + \text{error} \\
\Delta h &= \frac{\eta}{1+\eta}\Delta g + \text{error}
\end{aligned}
$$

By regressing Δh on Δg we get an estimate of $\eta/(1+\eta)$ as

$$
\widehat{\frac{\eta}{1+\eta}} = \frac{cov(\Delta h, \Delta g)}{var(\Delta g)} = \frac{.07}{.17} = \frac{7}{17}
$$

Solving for η gives an indirect least squares (ILS) estimate

$$
\hat{\eta} = 7/10 = .7 > 0.
$$

(*b*) Using the identity $g = w + h$, we can rewrite the regression as

$$
\begin{aligned}
\Delta h &= \eta \Delta w + \text{error} \\
&= \eta (\Delta g - \Delta h) + \text{error}
\end{aligned}
$$

By regressing Δh on $(\Delta g - \Delta h)$ we get

$$
\begin{aligned}
\tilde{\eta} &= \frac{cov(\Delta h, \Delta g - \Delta h)}{var(\Delta g - \Delta h)} \\
&= \frac{cov(\Delta h, \Delta g) - var(\Delta h)}{var(\Delta g) + var(\Delta h) - 2cov(\Delta g, \Delta h)} \\
&= \frac{.07 - .12}{.17 + .12 - 2 \times .07} \\
&= -\frac{1}{3} < 0
\end{aligned}
$$

If Δg were measured with error and the true $\eta > 0$, then the attenuation bias tends $\tilde{\eta}$ towards 0 but not negative. (However, annual earnings g is thought to be measured fairly accurately since one only needs to look at the tax form.) If Δh is measured with error, then in addition to the usual attenuation bias there is a "division bias" since Δh appears both as a regressand and regressor. When this division bias is large $\tilde{\eta}$ can be negative.

(*c*) The model $h_{i,t} = \overline{h}_i + \epsilon_{i,t}$ in first difference form is

$$
\Delta h_t = \Delta \epsilon_t = \epsilon_{i,t} - \epsilon_{i,t-1}
$$

The implied covariance structure (in first differences) is

$$
cov(\Delta h_t, \Delta h_{t-k}) = \begin{cases} 2\sigma^2 & (k = 0) \\ -\sigma^2 & (k = 1) \\ 0 & (k > 1) \end{cases}
$$

The GMM way to test these implications is to compare with the corresponding sample covariance. For instance, the implied *correlation* at lag 1 is -0.5 whereas the sample correlation at lag 1 is -0.25. (To formally test whether these two correlations are "close," we need an estimate of the fourth moments.)

Chapter 11

11.1.   This problem has appeared in a variety of other guises and has been a source of heated debated and confusion. If you are one of the confused (like myself), see J.P. Morgan, N.R. Chaganty, R.C. Dahiya, and M.J. Doviak "Let's Make a Deal: The Player's Dilemma," *The American Statistician*, Nov. 1991, v.45, N.4, 284–287.

(a, b) If she remains with her first choice, she wins if she had chosen the right door with probability 1/3. If she switches, she wins if she had chosen the wrong door with probability 2/3. (I assume the contestant is smart enough not to switch to the opened door.)

(c) I wrote the following mhall.ado file in *Stata*.

```
program define mhall
version 4.0
if "'1'"=="?" {
global S_1 "stick"
exit
}
drop _all
set obs 1
gen prize=int(uniform()*3)+1    /* choose door with prize */
gen first=int(uniform()*3)+1    /* contestant's 1st choice */
gen stick=(prize==first)        /* stick wins if 1st choice has prize, otherwise switch wins */
sum stick
post '1' _result(3)
end
```

The **simul** command gave the following result.

```
. simul mhall, reps(1000)

. ci stick
```

Variable	Obs	Mean	Std. Err.	[95% Conf. Interval]	
stick	1000	.336	.0149441	.3066745	.3653255

(d) We would like to have

$$2 \times s_p \times 1.96 = 0.02 \qquad \text{where } s_p^2 = p(1-p)/n.$$

Solving for n and noting that $p = 1/3$, we require

$$n = \left(\frac{2 \times 1.96}{0.02}\right)^2 p(1-p) = \left(\frac{2 \times 1.96}{0.02}\right)^2 \times \frac{1}{3} \times \frac{2}{3} \approx 8537$$

11.2.   We need to find a lower triangular 2×2 matrix A such that

$$AA' = \begin{bmatrix} a_{11} & 0 \\ a_{21} & a_{22} \end{bmatrix} \begin{bmatrix} a_{11} & a_{21} \\ 0 & a_{22} \end{bmatrix} = \begin{bmatrix} a_{11}^2 & a_{11}a_{21} \\ a_{11}a_{21} & a_{21}^2 + a_{22}^2 \end{bmatrix} = \begin{bmatrix} \sigma_1^2 & \sigma_{12} \\ \sigma_{12} & \sigma_2^2 \end{bmatrix} = \Sigma$$

Equating element by element of both sides we have

$$a_{11} = \sigma_1, \quad a_{21} = \frac{\sigma_{12}}{\sigma_1}, \quad a_{22} = \sigma_2\sqrt{1-\rho^2}$$

and

$$
\begin{aligned}
P &= \mu + AC \\
&= \begin{bmatrix} \mu_1 \\ \mu_2 \end{bmatrix} + \begin{bmatrix} a_{11} & 0 \\ a_{21} & a_{22} \end{bmatrix} \begin{bmatrix} c_1 \\ c_2 \end{bmatrix} \\
&= \begin{bmatrix} \mu_1 + c_1\sigma_1 \\ \mu_2 + (c_1\rho + c_2\sqrt{1-\rho^2})\sigma_2 \end{bmatrix}
\end{aligned}
$$

11.3.

$$
\begin{aligned}
\widehat{u}_t^2 &= (y_t - x_t b)^2 \\
&= (x_t\beta + u_t - x_t b)^2 \\
&= [x_t(\beta - b) + u_t]^2 \\
&= [-x_t(X'X)^{-1}X'u + u_t]^2 \\
&= x_t(X'X)^{-1}X'uu'X(X'X)^{-1}x_t' - 2x_t(X'X)^{-1}X'uu_t + u_t^2 \\
E(\widehat{u}_t^2) &= \sigma^2 x_t(X'X)^{-1}x_t' - 2\sigma^2 x_t(X'X)^{-1}x_t' + \sigma^2 \\
&= \sigma^2[1 - x_t(X'X)^{-1}x_t']
\end{aligned}
$$

11.4.   The (stacked) data ($\mathbf{x}$) were saved in 11_4.dta. The conventional t-test rejects the equality of means between the two groups.

```
. set maxvar 20 width 20
(1024k)

. use 11_4

. gen caff=(_n>10)

. ttest x, by(caff)

Variable |     Obs        Mean     Std. Dev.
---------+---------------------------------
       0 |      10       244.8     2.394438
       1 |      10       248.3     2.213594
---------+---------------------------------
combined |      20      246.55     2.874113

       Ho:  mean(x) = mean(y)   (assuming equal variances)
                 t = -3.39 with 18 d.f.
             Pr > |t| = 0.0032
```

To carry out the permutation test I wrote the following permut1.ado file in *Stata*.

```
program define permut1
version 4.0
if "`1'"=="?" {
global S_1 "diff"
exit
}
tempvar index
gen `index'=uniform()
sort `index'
qui sum x if _n<=10
local mean1=_result(3)
qui sum x if _n>10
local mean2=_result(3)
post `1' abs(`mean1'-`mean2')
end
```

The permutation test was carried out as follows:

```
. drop _all

. set maxvar 20 width 20
(1024k)

. use 11_4

. simul permut1, reps(10000)

. qui sum diff if diff>3.5

. dis "p-value="_result(1)/10000
p-value=.0029
```

Again we reject the equality of means between the two groups. Note that the p-value is close to the one obtained from the conventional t-test.

11.5. The following programs carry out the serial correlation permutation test for 100 Monte Carlo replications and 100 permutations (for each replication) from $\rho = 0$ to $\rho = 1$ in steps of .1. (Warning: these are not efficient programs; it may take a very long time. The *MATLAB* file runs faster than the *Stata* file.)

The following three ado-files in *Stata* store three variables in a datafile named dwtest.dta: **power_dw** (power of the DW-test for each ρ), **power_d** (power of the permutation test for each ρ), and **rho** (eleven values of ρ). At the *Stata* prompt simply type **permutdw**. When the simulation is done, bring in the **dwtest.dta** data file and analyze the results (e.g. plot the power function).

```
program define permutdw /* calls up dwtest.ado and permut2.ado */
version 4.0
tempname sim
postfile `sim' pow_dw pow_d rho using dwtest, replace
qui {
global M=100 /* set number of replications */
global L=100 /* set number of permutations */
global rho=0
while $rho <= 1.0 {
simul dwtest, r($M)
qui sum dwrej
local pow_dw=_result(3)
qui sum pval_d if pval_d<.05
local pow_d=_result(1)/$M
post `sim' `pow_dw' `pow_d' $rho
global rho=$rho+.1
```

```
}
}
postclose 'sim'
end

program define dwtest /* to be called by permutdw */
version 4.0
if "'1'"=="?" {
global S_1 "dwrej pval_d"
exit
}
drop _all
set obs 100
gen x=invnorm(uniform())
gen v=invnorm(uniform())
gen y=0
replace y=$rho*y[_n-1]+v if _n>1
qui regdw y x /* note y=epsilon */
local dwrej=($S_1<1.522) /* lower bound from table */
predict ehat, resid
gen ehatlag=ehat[_n-1]
qui corr ehat ehatlag
local ar1=_result(4)
simul permut2, reps($L) /* premute 'L' times */
qui sum if par1>'ar1'
post '1' 'dwrej' _result(1)/$L
end

program define permut2 /* to be called by dwtest */
version 4.0
if "'1'"=="?" {
global S_1 "par1"
exit
}
tempvar ind rlag
gen 'ind'=uniform()
sort 'ind'
gen 'rlag'=ehat[_n-1]
qui corr ehat 'rlag'
post '1' _result(4)
end
```

The following m-file in *MATLAB* plots the power function of the DW-test and the permutation test.

```
% exercise 11_5, permutate DW

power=zeros(1,11);
powerdw=zeros(1,11);

for rho=0:0.1:1

n=100;              % number of replications
m=100;              % number of permutations

simd=zeros(m,1);
dw=zeros(n,1);
d=zeros(n,1);
pval=zeros(n,1);
e=zeros(100,1);
elag=zeros(100,1);
```

```
for j=1:n
v = randn(100,2);      % generate the series
u = v(:,1);
x = v(:,2);
e(1)=u(1);
for i=2:100
e(i) = rho*e(i-1) + u(i);
end

rhs=[ones(size(x)) x];     % run the regression
beta = rhs\e;              % and compute dw and d
res = e-rhs*beta;
reslag(2:100,:) = res(1:99,:);
dres = res-reslag;
dres = dres(2:100,:);
dw(j) = sum(dres.^2)/sum(res.^2);
d(j) = sum(res.*reslag)/sum(res.^2);

for k=1:m                  % permutation test
b=rand(100,1);
[b,index]=sort(b);
dog=res(index,:);  % dog is the permutation of res
doglag(2:100,:) = dog(1:99,:);
%ddog = dog-doglag;
%ddog = ddog(2:100,:);
simd(k) = sum(dog.*doglag)/sum(dog.^2); % simd is d_{1}
end

i=find(simd>d(j));         % compute the percentile of d
num=zeros(m,1);
num(i)=ones(size(i));
pval(j)=sum(num)/m;
end

i=find(dw<1.522);          % critical value of DW
num=zeros(n,1);            % Savin-White, EM III, Table B-5, p.554
num(i)=ones(size(i));      % compute the power of DW
powerdw(rho*10+1)=sum(num)/n;

i=find(pval<0.05);
num=zeros(n,1);
num(i)=ones(size(i));
power(rho*10+1)=sum(num)/n;

end

rho=[0:0.1:1];
plot(rho,powerdw,'--',rho,power,'-')
```

The power functions from one execution is shown in Figure 11.1. The permutation test dominates the DW-test for small ρ.

11.6. There are two ways you can simulate the distribution of the t-statistics: by permutation (without replacement) and by bootstrapping (with replacement).

To use the following ado-files in *Stata* you first need to save the (stacked) data (with a variable name x) in 11_5.dta. The first program does the permutation, while the second program does the bootstrapping.

```
program define permut3
```

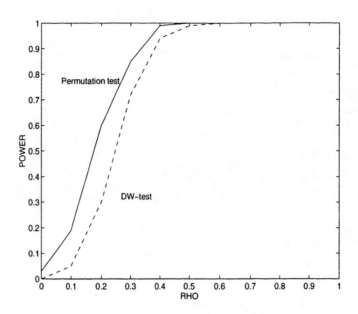

Figure 11.1: Power functions of the DW-test and the permutation test

```
version 4.0
if "'1'"=="?" {
use 11_6, clear
global S_1 "t_stat"
exit
}
tempvar index nj
gen 'index'=uniform()
sort 'index'
gen 'nj'=(_n<=33)
qui ttest x, by('nj')
post '1' $S_6
end

program define boot3
version 4.0
if "'1'"=="?" {
use 11_6, clear
gen nj=(_n<=33)
global S_1 "t_stat"
exit
}
tempvar x2 index
gen 'x2'=x
gen 'index'=int(40*uniform())+1
local i=1
while 'i'<=40 {
if 'i'~='index'['i'] {
replace 'x2'=x['index'] in 'i'/'i'
}
local i='i'+1
}
qui ttest 'x2', by(nj)
```

```
post '1' $S_6
end
```

The resulting distribution of the t-statistics (from 1000 replications) was estimated using a Gaussian kernel and a rectangular kernel.

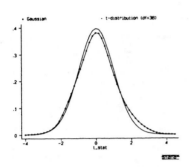
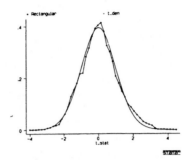

Figure 11.2: Kernel density estimates of the distribution of t-statistics from permutated samples

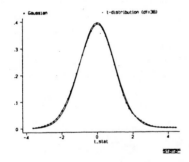
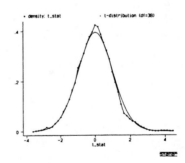

Figure 11.3: Kernel density estimates of the distribution of t-statistics from bootstrapped samples

Chapter 12

12.1.

(a) Eq. (12.57) can be written as

$$y_i = X_i\beta + \epsilon_i, \quad \text{for } i = 1, 2, \ldots, N \qquad \text{where } E(\epsilon_i \epsilon_i') = \sigma^2 G_N$$

This is a SUR system with N equations, each with T observations. Appendix 9.1 shows that $b_{GLS} = b_{OLS}$ if the regressors X_i in all N equations are the same. This is the case since $X_i = [1 \ U_t]$ for all i.

(b)

$$
\begin{aligned}
X'X &= [x_1 i' \ \cdots \ x_T i']
\begin{bmatrix}
i x_1' \\
\vdots \\
i x_T'
\end{bmatrix} \\
&= x_1 i' i x_1' + \cdots + x_T i' i x_T' \\
&= N(x_1 x_1' + \cdots + x_T x_T') \\
&= N \sum x_t x_t'
\end{aligned}
$$

and so

$$V_{OLS}^* = \sigma^2 (X'X)^{-1} = \frac{\sigma^2}{N} \left(\sum x_t x_t' \right)^{-1}$$

(c)

$$
\begin{aligned}
b_{OLS} &= \beta + (X'X)^{-1} X' \epsilon \\
var(b_{OLS}) &= \sigma^2 (X'X)^{-1} X' G X (X'X)^{-1}
\end{aligned}
$$

where

$$
\begin{aligned}
X'GX &= [x_1 i' \ \cdots \ x_T i']
\begin{bmatrix}
G_N & & 0 \\
& \ddots & \\
0 & & G_N
\end{bmatrix}
\begin{bmatrix}
i x_1' \\
\vdots \\
i x_T'
\end{bmatrix} \\
&= x_1 i' G_N i x_1' + \cdots + x_T i' G_N i x_T'
\end{aligned}
$$

and

$$i'G_N i = i'[(1-\rho)I_N + \rho ii']i$$
$$= (1-\rho)i'i + \rho i'ii'i$$
$$= N(1-\rho) + N^2\rho$$

so that

$$X'GX = N(1-\rho+N\rho)\sum x_t x_t'.$$

Then

$$var(b_{OLS}) = \sigma^2 (X'X)^{-1} X'GX (X'X)^{-1}$$
$$= \sigma^2 \left(N\sum x_t x_t'\right)^{-1} N(1-\rho+N\rho)\left(\sum x_t x_t'\right)\left(N\sum x_t x_t'\right)^{-1}$$
$$= \frac{(1-\rho+N\rho)\sigma^2}{N}\left(\sum x_t x_t'\right)^{-1}$$
$$= (1-\rho+N\rho)V_{OLS}^*$$

12.2.

(a) From the first step regression, we get

$$\widehat{\delta} = (D'D)^{-1}D'y = \overline{y}_{\cdot t}$$

which are the means of y_i for each period. Then the second stage regression has the form

$$\overline{y}_{\cdot t} = x_t'\widetilde{b} + \text{resid} = \bar{x}_{\cdot t}\widetilde{b} + \text{resid}$$

since all i have the same x_t in each period. This shows that $\widetilde{b}$ is just the between estimator, which we know is consistent. To see this let $x = [x_1 \cdots x_T]'$, a $T \times 2$ matrix. Noting that $X = Dx$,

$$\widetilde{b} = (x'x)^{-1}x'\widehat{\delta}$$
$$= (x'x)^{-1}x'(D'D)^{-1}D'(X\beta + \epsilon)$$
$$= (x'x)^{-1}x'(D'D)^{-1}D'Dx\beta + (x'x)^{-1}x'(D'D)^{-1}D'\epsilon$$
$$= \beta + (x'x)^{-1}x'(D'D)^{-1}D'\epsilon$$
$$\xrightarrow{p} \beta$$

(b) The second stage regression is a bivariate regression of $\overline{y}_{\cdot t}$ on U_t. Since the left-hand side is a mean, its variation gets small as N gets big. Therefore the second stage equation will hold nearly exactly as an identity and $R^2 \to 1$ *if the model is correctly specified.*

12.3. Note that

$$cov(\nu_{i,t}, \nu_{j,s}) = \begin{cases} \sigma_\mu^2 + \sigma_\lambda^2 + \sigma_\epsilon^2 & \text{if } i=j \text{ and } t=s \\ \sigma_\mu^2 & \text{if } i=j \text{ and } t\neq s \\ \sigma_\lambda^2 & \text{if } i\neq j \text{ and } t=s \\ 0 & \text{otherwise} \end{cases}$$

We can write out the covariance matrix as

$$V = E(\nu\nu') = \begin{bmatrix} D & F & \cdots & F \\ F & D & & F \\ \vdots & & \ddots & \vdots \\ F & \cdots & F & D \end{bmatrix} = I_N \otimes (D - F) + J_N \otimes F$$

where

$$D_T = \begin{bmatrix} \sigma^2 & \sigma_\mu^2 & \cdots & \sigma_\mu^2 \\ \sigma_\mu^2 & \sigma^2 & & \sigma_\mu^2 \\ \vdots & & \ddots & \vdots \\ \sigma_\mu^2 & \cdots & \sigma_\mu^2 & \sigma^2 \end{bmatrix} = \sigma^2 \begin{bmatrix} 1 & \rho & \cdots & \rho \\ \rho & 1 & & \rho \\ \vdots & & \ddots & \vdots \\ \rho & \cdots & \rho & 1 \end{bmatrix} = \sigma^2[(1-\rho)I_T + \rho J_T]$$

and

$$F_T = \begin{bmatrix} \sigma_\lambda^2 & \cdots & 0 \\ \vdots & \ddots & \vdots \\ 0 & \cdots & \sigma_\lambda^2 \end{bmatrix} = \sigma^2 \begin{bmatrix} w & \cdots & 0 \\ \vdots & \ddots & \vdots \\ 0 & \cdots & w \end{bmatrix} = \sigma^2 w I_T$$

Therefore[1]

$$\begin{aligned} V &= I_N \otimes (D - F) + J_N \otimes F \\ &= I_N \otimes [\sigma^2(1-\rho-w)I_T + \sigma^2\rho J_T] + J_N \otimes \sigma^2 w I_T \\ &= \sigma^2(1-\rho-w)I_N \otimes I_T + \sigma^2\rho I_N \otimes J_T + \sigma^2 w J_N \otimes I_T \\ &= \sigma^2[(1-\rho-w)I_{NT} + \rho A + w B] \end{aligned}$$

12.4. Let the model be

$$y_{i,t} = x_{i,t}\beta + \nu_{i,t} = x_{i,t}\beta + \mu_i + \lambda_t + \epsilon_{i,t}$$

Possible estimators of the variance of the error components are tabulated below.

Model	Residual variance
$\overline{y}_{i\cdot} = \overline{x}_{i\cdot}\beta + \mu_i + \overline{\lambda} + \overline{\epsilon}_{i\cdot}$	$\widehat{\sigma}_\mu^2 + (\widehat{\sigma}_\lambda^2 + \widehat{\sigma}_\epsilon^2)/T$
$\overline{y}_{\cdot t} = \overline{x}_{\cdot t}\beta + \overline{\mu} + \lambda_t + \overline{\epsilon}_{\cdot t}$	$\widehat{\sigma}_\lambda^2 + (\widehat{\sigma}_\mu^2 + \widehat{\sigma}_\epsilon^2)/N$
$y_{i,t} - \overline{y}_{i\cdot} = (x_{i,t} - \overline{x}_{i\cdot})\beta + \lambda_t - \overline{\lambda} + \epsilon_{i,t} - \overline{\epsilon}_{i\cdot}$	$(\widehat{\sigma}_\lambda^2 + \widehat{\sigma}_\epsilon^2)(T-1)/T$
$y_{i,t} - \overline{y}_{\cdot t} = (x_{i,t} - \overline{x}_{\cdot t})\beta + \mu_i - \overline{\mu} + \epsilon_{i,t} - \overline{\epsilon}_{\cdot t}$	$(\widehat{\sigma}_\mu^2 + \widehat{\sigma}_\epsilon^2)(N-1)/N$
$y_{i,t} - \overline{y}_{i\cdot} - \overline{y}_{\cdot t} + \overline{\overline{y}} = (x_{i,t} - \overline{x}_{i\cdot} - \overline{x}_{\cdot t} + \overline{\overline{x}})\beta$ $+\epsilon_{i,t} - \overline{\epsilon}_{i\cdot} - \overline{\epsilon}_{\cdot t} + \overline{\overline{\epsilon}}$	$\widehat{\sigma}_\epsilon^2[1 + (N-1)^2][1 + (T-1)^2]/(NT)^2$

Any three models can be used to solve for the three unknowns $\widehat{\sigma}_\mu^2$, $\widehat{\sigma}_\lambda^2$, $\widehat{\sigma}_\epsilon^2$. (Note that in finite samples, some of the estimates might become negative.)

---

[1] I use the fact that

$$\begin{aligned} A \otimes (B + C) &= A \otimes B + A \otimes C \\ A \otimes kB &= kA \otimes B \end{aligned}$$

where A, B, C are matrices and k is a scalar.

12.5.   We consider the standard case where we fix T and take the plim as $N \to \infty$.

(a)

$$b_{OLS} = (x'x)^{-1}x'y$$

$$\text{plim}\,\frac{x'x}{N} = \text{plim}\sum_t \frac{x'_t x_t}{N}$$

$$= T(\sigma_{x^*}^2 + \sigma_u^2)$$

$$\text{plim}\,\frac{x'y}{N} = \text{plim}\sum_t \frac{x'_t y_t}{N}$$

$$= \text{plim}\sum_t \frac{(x_t^* + u_t)'(\alpha^* + \beta x_t^* + \epsilon_t)}{N}$$

$$= T(\sigma_{x^* \alpha} + \beta\sigma_{x^*}^2)$$

$$\text{plim}\,b_{OLS} = \frac{\sigma_{x^* \alpha} + \beta\sigma_{x^*}^2}{\sigma_{x^*}^2 + \sigma_u^2}$$

$$= \beta + \frac{\sigma_{x^* \alpha}}{\sigma_{x^*}^2 + \sigma_u^2} - \frac{\beta\sigma_u^2}{\sigma_{x^*}^2 + \sigma_u^2}$$

This is Eq. (12.42); the middle term is the bias due to the fixed effect and the last term is the attenuation bias due to measurement error.

(b) Let $y_{W,t}$ and $x_{W,t}$ be $n \times 1$ vectors with i-th elements

$$y_{i,t} - \bar{y}_{i\cdot} = \beta(x_{i,t}^* - \bar{x}_{i\cdot}^*) + \epsilon_{i,t} - \bar{\epsilon}_{i\cdot}$$

$$x_{i,t} - \bar{x}_{i\cdot} = x_{i,t}^* - \bar{x}_{i\cdot}^* + u_{i,t} - \bar{u}_{i\cdot}$$

The within estimator (the fixed effect estimator) is

$$b_W = (x'_W x_w)^{-1} x'_W y_W$$

where

$$\text{plim}\,\frac{x'_W x_W}{N} = \text{plim}\sum_t \frac{x'_{W,t} x_{W,t}}{N}$$

$$= (T-1)(\sigma_{x^*}^2 + \sigma_u^2)$$

$$\text{plim}\,\frac{x'_W y_W}{N} = \text{plim}\sum_t \frac{x'_{W,t} y_{W,t}}{N}$$

$$= (T-1)\beta\sigma_{x^*}^2$$

$$\text{plim}\,b_W = \frac{\beta\sigma_{x^*}^2}{\sigma_{x^*}^2 + \sigma_u^2}$$

$$= \beta - \frac{\beta\sigma_u^2}{\sigma_{x^*}^2 + \sigma_u^2}$$

The first difference estimator is

$$b_{FD} = ((x_{i,t} - \bar{x}_{i,t-1})'(x_{i,t} - \bar{x}_{i,t-1}))^{-1}(x_{i,t} - \bar{x}_{i,t-1})'(y_{i,t} - \bar{y}_{i,t-1})$$

Since x^* is assumed *iid*, $\rho = 0$ in Eq. (12.38) and

$$\text{plim}\, b_{FD} = \text{plim}\, b_W.$$

(c) Let y_B and x_B be $n \times 1$ vectors with i-th elements

$$\begin{aligned}
\overline{y}_{i\cdot} &= \alpha_i^* + \beta \overline{x}_{i\cdot}^* + \overline{\epsilon}_{i\cdot} \\
\overline{x}_{i\cdot} &= \overline{x}_{i\cdot}^* + \overline{u}_{i\cdot}
\end{aligned}$$

The between estimator is

$$\begin{aligned}
b_B &= (x_B' x_B)^{-1} x_B' y_B \\
\text{plim}\, \frac{x_B' x_B}{N} &= \frac{1}{T}(\sigma_{x^*}^2 + \sigma_u^2) \\
\text{plim}\, \frac{x_B' y_B}{N} &= \frac{1}{T}(T\sigma_{x^* \alpha} + \beta \sigma_{x^*}^2) \\
\text{plim}\, b_B &= \frac{T\sigma_{x^* \alpha} + \beta \sigma_{x^*}^2}{\sigma_{x^*}^2 + \sigma_u^2} \\
&= \beta + \frac{T\sigma_{x^* \alpha}}{\sigma_{x^*}^2 + \sigma_u^2} - \frac{\beta \sigma_u^2}{\sigma_{x^*}^2 + \sigma_u^2}
\end{aligned}$$

Note that the between estimator is consistent when we fix N and let $T \to \infty$. The intuition is that in this case the between estimator can be considered as a 2SLS estimator where the individual specific dummies are the instruments. Note that these fixed effects satisfy the conditions for instruments: correlated with x^* but uncorrelated with ϵ.

(d) The random effects estimator given in Eqs. (12.17), (12.18) is

$$b_{RE} = (x_R' x_R)^{-1} x_R' y_R$$

where y_R and x_R are $nT \times 1$ vectors with it-th elements

$$\begin{aligned}
y_{i,t} - \lambda \overline{y}_{i\cdot} &= (1-\lambda)\alpha^* + \beta(x_{i,t}^* - \lambda \overline{x}_{i\cdot}^*) + \epsilon_{i,t} - \lambda \overline{\epsilon}_{i\cdot} \\
x_{i,t} - \lambda \overline{x}_{i\cdot} &= x_{i,t}^* - \lambda \overline{x}_{i\cdot}^* + u_{i,t} - \lambda \overline{u}_{i\cdot}
\end{aligned}$$

where $\lambda = 1 - \theta$ and θ are defined in Eq. (12.12). We have

$$\begin{aligned}
\text{plim}\, \frac{x_R' x_R}{N} &= \text{plim}\, \sum_t \frac{x_{R,t}' x_{R,t}}{N} \\
&= \left(\frac{(T-\lambda)^2 + \lambda^2(T-1)}{T} \right)(\sigma_{x^*}^2 + \sigma_u^2) \\
\text{plim}\, \frac{x_R' y_R}{N} &= \text{plim}\, \sum_t \frac{x_{R,t}' y_{R,t}}{N} \\
&= T(1-\lambda)^2 \sigma_{x^* \alpha} + \left(\frac{(T-\lambda)^2 + \lambda^2(T-1)}{T} \right) \beta \sigma_{x^*}^2 \\
\text{plim}\, b_{RE} &= \beta + \frac{T^2(1-\lambda)^2}{(T-\lambda)^2 + \lambda^2(T-1)} \frac{\sigma_{x^* \alpha}}{\sigma_{x^*}^2 + \sigma_u^2} - \frac{\beta \sigma_u^2}{\sigma_{x^*}^2 + \sigma_u^2}
\end{aligned}$$

Note that even when $\sigma_u^2 = 0$ (no measurement error), the bias does not disappear; applying the random effects estimator to a fixed effect model results in bias.

12.6. From Eq. (12.12), we have

$$
\begin{aligned}
\Sigma^{-1} &= \Sigma^{-\frac{1}{2}}\Sigma^{-\frac{1}{2}} \\
&= \frac{1}{\sigma_\eta^2}\left(I - \frac{2(1-\theta)}{T}ii' + \left(\frac{1-\theta}{T}\right)^2 ii'ii'\right) \\
&= \frac{1}{\sigma_\eta^2}\left[I + \left(\frac{\theta^2-1}{T}\right)ii'\right] \\
\Sigma^{-1}\Sigma &= \frac{1}{\sigma_\eta^2}\left[I + \left(\frac{\theta^2-1}{T}\right)ii'\right](\sigma_\eta^2 I + \sigma_\alpha^2 ii') \\
&= I + \left(\frac{\theta^2-1}{T} + \frac{\theta^2\sigma_\alpha^2}{\sigma_\eta^2}\right)ii'
\end{aligned}
$$

Since the last expression must be identically equal to I, the term in parentheses must be identically equal to 0. Solving for θ yields the expression given in Eq. (12.12).

12.7. Note that

$$
E(\epsilon_{i,t}\epsilon_{j,t-k}) = E[\epsilon_{j,t-k}(\rho_i^k\epsilon_{i,t-k} + \text{lagged terms of } \nu_{i,t})] = \rho_i^k\sigma_{ij}
$$

Therefore we can write the covariance matrix as

$$
\Omega = E(\epsilon\epsilon') = \begin{bmatrix} \Omega_{11} & \cdots & \Omega_{1N} \\ \vdots & \ddots & \vdots \\ \Omega_{N1} & \cdots & \Omega_{NN} \end{bmatrix}
$$

where

$$
\Omega_{ij} = \sigma_{ij}\begin{bmatrix} 1 & \rho_j & \cdots & & \rho_j^{T-1} \\ \rho_i & 1 & \rho_j & \cdots & \\ \vdots & & \ddots & & \vdots \\ & & & 1 & \rho_j \\ \rho_i^{T-1} & & \cdots & \rho_i & 1 \end{bmatrix}
$$

is a $T \times T$ matrix.

FGLS requires a consistent estimate of Ω, i.e. consistent estimates of ρ_i and σ_{ij}. This can be obtained by the following procedure.

(1) Run pooled OLS and get the residuals $e_{i,t}$.

(2) Regress $e_{i,t}$ on $e_{i,t-1}$ to get $\hat{\rho}_i$. (This is a consistent estimate of ρ unless there are lagged y's in X.)

(3) Remove autocorrelation by the transformation

$$
\begin{aligned}
y_{i,t}^* &= y_{i,t} - \hat{\rho}_i y_{i,t-1} \\
x_{i,t}^* &= x_{i,t} - \hat{\rho}_i x_{i,t-1}
\end{aligned}
$$

and regress y^* on X^* to get the residuals e^*. This transformation throws away the first observation. When T is small, as is typically the case, we can transform the first observation as

$$
\begin{aligned}
y_{i,1}^* &= \sqrt{1-\hat{\rho}_i^2}\, y_{i,1} \\
x_{i,1}^* &= \sqrt{1-\hat{\rho}_i^2}\, x_{i,1}
\end{aligned}
$$

(4) To get an estimate of σ_{ij}, note that

$$
\begin{aligned}
\sigma_{ij} &= E(\epsilon_{i,t}\epsilon_{j,t}) \\
&= E[(\rho_i\epsilon_{i,t-1} + \nu_{i,t})(\rho_j\epsilon_{j,t-1} + \nu_{j,t})] \\
&= \rho_i\rho_j E(\epsilon_{i,t-1}\epsilon_{j,t-1}) + E(\nu_{i,t}\nu_{j,t}) \\
&= \rho_i\rho_j\sigma_{ij} + E(\nu_{i,t}\nu_{j,t}) \\
&= \frac{E(\nu_{i,t}\nu_{j,t})}{1 - \rho_i\rho_j}
\end{aligned}
$$

Therefore we can estimate σ_{ij} by

$$
s_{ij} = \frac{(\sum_t e_{i,t}^* e_{j,t}^*)/T}{1 - \widehat{\rho}_i\widehat{\rho}_j}
$$

(5) Use $\widehat{\rho}_i, s_{ij}$ to construct an estimate $\widehat{\Omega}^{-1}$ and compute

$$
b_{GLS} = (X'\widehat{\Omega}^{-1}X)^{-1}X'\widehat{\Omega}^{-1}y
$$

Chapter 13

13.1. The log likelihood of the logit and its derivatives are given by

$$\ell = \sum_i \left(y_i \ln \left(\frac{e^{x_i\beta}}{1 + e^{x_i\beta}} \right) + (1 - y_i) \ln \left(\frac{1}{1 + e^{x_i\beta}} \right) \right)$$

$$= \sum \left(y_i x_i \beta - \ln(1 + e^{x_i\beta}) \right)$$

$$\frac{\partial \ell}{\partial \beta} = \sum \left(y_i x_i - \left(\frac{e^{x_i\beta}}{1 + e^{x_i\beta}} \right) x_i \right)$$

$$\frac{\partial^2 \ell}{\partial \beta \partial \beta'} = -\sum \frac{e^{x_i\beta}}{(1 + e^{x_i\beta})^2} x_i x_i'$$

The last expression shows that the matrix of second derivatives is negative semi-definite and hence the logit has a globally concave log likelihood.

13.2. For the linear probability model,

$$\widehat{p}_i = X_i b$$

$$X_i' \widehat{p}_i = X_i' X_i b$$

$$\sum X_i' \widehat{p}_i = \sum X_i' X_i b$$

$$= \sum X_i' y_i$$

where the last equality follows from the normal equations of least squares. If the first column of X is a constant (one), then the first row of the last expression gives

$$\sum_i \widehat{p}_i = \sum_i y_i$$

For the logit,

$$\widehat{p}_i = \frac{e^{X_i b}}{1 + e^{X_i b}}$$

$$X_i' \widehat{p}_i = X_i' \left(\frac{e^{X_i b}}{1 + e^{X_i b}} \right)$$

$$\sum X_i' \widehat{p}_i = \sum X_i' \left(\frac{e^{X_i b}}{1 + e^{X_i b}} \right)$$

$$= \sum X_i' y_i$$

117

where the last equality follows from the first order conditions for b_{MLE} (see the expression of the score in Problem 13.1). If the first column of X is a constant (one), then the first row of the last expression gives

$$\sum_i \widehat{p}_i = \sum_i y_i$$

13.3.   Denote the LR test statistic as

$$
\begin{aligned}
LR &= 2\Big(\sum_j (n_j p_j \ln p_j + n_j(1-p_j)\ln(1-p_j)) \\
&\qquad - \sum_j \Big(n_j p_j \ln F(X_j\widehat{\beta}) + n_j(1-p_j)\ln(1-F(X_j\widehat{\beta}))\Big)\Big) \\
&= 2\big(\ell_0(p) - \ell_1(\widehat{\beta})\big)
\end{aligned}
$$

Taking a second order Taylor expansion of ℓ_0 around $p = \pi$ gives

$$\ell_0(p) = \sum\big(n_j p_j \ln \pi_j + n_j(1-p_j)\ln(1-\pi_j) + \frac{1}{2}\frac{n_j(p_j - \pi_j)^2}{\pi_j(1-\pi_j)}\big)$$

where the second order term is distributed χ^2 with J degrees of freedom.

Similarly, taking a second order Taylor expansion of $\ell_1(\widehat{\beta})$ around $\widehat{\beta} = \beta$ gives

$$\ell_1(\widehat{\beta}) = \ell_1(\beta) + \frac{\partial \ell_1}{\partial \beta}(\widehat{\beta} - \beta) + \frac{1}{2}(\widehat{\beta} - \beta)'\frac{\partial^2 \ell_1}{\partial \beta \partial \beta'}(\widehat{\beta} - \beta)$$

The first order term vanishes from the first order conditions of MLE and the second term is χ^2 with K degrees of freedom. Since the constant terms of ℓ_0 and ℓ_1 cancel out we have

$$LR \sim \chi^2(J - K).$$

13.4.

(*a*)

$$
\begin{aligned}
E(y|x=0) &= \beta_0 \\
E(y|x=1) &= \beta_0 + \beta_1 \\
&= E(y|x=0) + \beta_1
\end{aligned}
$$

$\widehat{\beta}_0 = 0.6$ is the mean of y conditional on $x = 0$ and $\widehat{\beta}_0 + \widehat{\beta}_1 = 0.4$ is the mean of y conditional on $x = 1$. The predicted values of y are

$$\widehat{y} = 0.6 - 0.2x = \begin{cases} 0.6 & \text{if } x = 0 \\ 0.4 & \text{if } x = 1 \end{cases}$$

(*b*) The log likelihood of the probit and its score are

$$
\begin{aligned}
\ell &= \sum_i \{y_i \ln \Phi(b_0 + b_1 x_i) + (1 - y_i)\ln[1 - \Phi(b_0 + b_1 x_i)]\} \\
&= \sum_{x=0,y=0} + \sum_{x=0,y=1} + \sum_{x=1,y=0} + \sum_{x=1,y=1}
\end{aligned}
$$

$$\begin{aligned}
&= 40\ln[1-\Phi(b_0)] + 60\ln\Phi(b_0) + 60\ln[1-\Phi(b_0+b_1)] + 40\ln\Phi(b_0+b_1) \\
\frac{\partial \ell}{\partial b_0} &= -\frac{40\phi(b_0)}{1-\Phi(b_0)} + \frac{60\phi(b_0)}{\Phi(b_0)} - \frac{60\phi(b_0+b_1)}{1-\Phi(b_0+b_1)} + \frac{40\phi(b_0+b_1)}{\Phi(b_0+b_1)} \\
\frac{\partial \ell}{\partial b_1} &= -\frac{60\phi(b_0+b_1)}{1-\Phi(b_0+b_1)} + \frac{40\phi(b_0+b_1)}{\Phi(b_0+b_1)}
\end{aligned}$$

Setting the scores equal to zero (the first order conditions) and simplifying yield

$$\begin{cases} \Phi(b_0+b_1) &= 0.4 \\ \Phi(b_0) &= 0.6 \end{cases} \quad \text{or} \quad \begin{cases} b_0 &= \Phi^{-1}(0.6) = 0.26 \\ b_1 &= \Phi^{-1}(0.4) - \Phi^{-1}(0.6) = -0.52 \end{cases}$$

The predicted values are

$$\hat{y} = \widehat{\Pr}(y=1) = \Phi(0.26 - 0.52x) = \begin{cases} 0.6 & \text{if } x = 0 \\ 0.4 & \text{if } x = 1 \end{cases}$$

13.5.

(a, b) For any cumulative distribution function F, the likelihood is given by

$$L = \Pr(y_1)\Pr(y_2)\cdots\Pr(y_n) = \prod_{y=k} F(X\beta) \prod_{y=0}(1 - F(X\beta))$$

where k is any number that y takes on. This shows that the MLE does not depend on the particular value that y takes on. This is true for any distribution function F.

(c) For the linear probability model

$$b_k = (X'X)^{-1}X'y_k = (X'X)^{-1}X'ky_1 = kb_1$$

where b_k denotes the estimate of β when $y = k$. Thus the coefficients will be k times that of the coefficients when $y = 1$. When $y = 1$ the conditional expectation of y and $\Pr(y = 1)$ are the same; the coefficient measures the marginal contribution to these two quantities. When $y = k$, however, the conditional expectation of y is k times $\Pr(y = k)$; the coefficient measures the marginal contribution to the conditional expectation and k times $\Pr(y = k)$.

13.6.   A uniform distribution on the interval $[c, d]$ has a cumulative distribution function of the form

$$F(x) = \begin{cases} 0 & \text{if } x < c \\ (x - c)/(d - c) & \text{if } c \le x < d \\ 1 & \text{if } d \le x \end{cases}$$

The model is then (note that the distribution is symmetric around $x = (c+d)/2$)

$$\begin{aligned}
\Pr(y_i = 1) &= \Pr(\epsilon > -X_i\beta) \\
&= 1 - F(-X_i\beta) \\
&= \begin{cases} 1 & \text{if } -X_i\beta < c \\ (d + X_i\beta)/(d - c) & \text{if } c \le -X_i\beta < d \\ 0 & \text{if } d \le X_i\beta \end{cases}
\end{aligned}$$

Note that this the linear probability model, except that it is forced to be 0 or 1 outside the relevant range.

Consider estimating this model. The likelihood function is given by

$$L = \Pr(y_1)\Pr(y_2)\cdots\Pr(y_n) = \prod \left(\frac{X_i\beta - c}{d - c} \right)$$

Note that this likelihood function is monotonically increasing in β (assuming X is positive) and the MLE must be at an endpoint. In fact, the uniform distribution is a well known example that violates the regularity conditions required for MLE to have "nice" properties. (See Problem 5.2.)

13.7.   The log likelihoods are

$$\ell_0 = \sum_{y>0} \frac{(y - x\beta)^2}{\sigma^2} + \sum_{y=0} \ln\left(1 - \Phi\left(\frac{x\beta}{\sigma}\right)\right) + \text{constant}$$

$$\ell_c = \sum_{z>c} \frac{(z - x\beta)^2}{\sigma^2} + \sum_{z=c} \ln\left(1 - \Phi\left(\frac{x\beta}{\sigma}\right)\right) + \text{constant}$$

where the subscript denotes the truncation level. If the Tobit specification is correct, both estimates are consistent and should be "close" to each other. However, by truncating more data ($c > 0$) we are throwing away information, which results in loss of efficiency; when c becomes large, most observations get bunched in the second term of ℓ_c. If there is heteroskedasticity in the Tobit, change in the truncation level can have more serious effects; by truncating the low (or high) variance group, the estimated coefficients can even change signs.

13.8.

```
. use cps88

. reg lnwage potexp exp2 grade married union

  Source |       SS       df       MS                  Number of obs =    1000
---------+------------------------------               F( 5,   994) =  111.67
   Model |  114.08409      5  22.8168179               Prob > F      =  0.0000
Residual |  203.09014    994  .204316036               R-squared     =  0.3597
---------+------------------------------               Adj R-squared =  0.3565
   Total |  317.174229   999  .317491721               Root MSE      =  .45201

---------------------------------------------------------------------------
  lnwage |    Coef.   Std. Err.       t    P>|t|    [95% Conf. Interval]
---------+-----------------------------------------------------------------
  potexp |  .0390884   .0045126     8.662   0.000    .0302332    .0479437
    exp2 | -.0005216   .0000946    -5.514   0.000   -.0007072   -.0003359
   grade |  .0936657   .0058379    16.045   0.000    .0822098    .1051217
 married |  .0966236   .0342586     2.820   0.005    .029396     .1638511
   union |  .1752994   .035727      4.907   0.000    .1051905    .2454084
   _cons |  .4897457   .0840693     5.825   0.000    .324772     .6547195
---------------------------------------------------------------------------

. tobit lnwage potexp exp2 grade married union, ll(1.87)

Tobit Estimates                                        Number of obs =    1000
                                                       chi2(5)       =  441.74
                                                       Prob > chi2   =  0.0000
Log Likelihood = -665.98359                            Pseudo R2     =  0.2490

---------------------------------------------------------------------------
  lnwage |    Coef.   Std. Err.       t    P>|t|    [95% Conf. Interval]
```

```
---------+-------------------------------------------------------------------
 potexp |   .0402208    .004887     8.230   0.000      .0306308    .0498109
   exp2 |   -.000515   .0001012    -5.089   0.000     -.0007135   -.0003164
  grade |   .1005957   .0062803    16.018   0.000      .0882714    .1129199
married |    .083644   .0358606     2.332   0.020       .013273     .154015
  union |   .1821755   .0364832     4.993   0.000      .1105827    .2537683
  _cons |   .3762287   .0945738     3.978   0.000      .1906418    .5618156
---------+-------------------------------------------------------------------
    _se |   .4544646    .012187              (Ancillary parameter)
-----------------------------------------------------------------------------
```

Obs. summary: 245 left-censored observations at lnwage<=1.87
                     755 uncensored observations

. tobit lnwage potexp exp2 grade married union, ll(3)

Tobit Estimates   Number of obs =   1000
                                               chi2(5)   =   163.68
                                               Prob > chi2   =   0.0000
Log Likelihood = -212.0478   Pseudo R2   =   0.2785


```
-----------------------------------------------------------------------------
 lnwage |    Coef.   Std. Err.      t     P>|t|     [95% Conf. Interval]
---------+-------------------------------------------------------------------
 potexp |   .0152265   .0092046     1.654   0.098     -.0028362    .0332891
   exp2 |  -.0000318   .0001888    -0.168   0.866     -.0004022    .0003387
  grade |   .1187442   .0140933     8.426   0.000      .0910882    .1464002
married |   .0913564   .0654943     1.395   0.163     -.0371665    .2198792
  union |  -.0883568   .0683848    -1.292   0.197     -.2225519    .0458382
  _cons |   .4416003   .2692408     1.640   0.101     -.0867445    .9699452
---------+-------------------------------------------------------------------
    _se |   .4348143   .0359208              (Ancillary parameter)
-----------------------------------------------------------------------------
```

Obs. summary: 898 left-censored observations at lnwage<=3
                     102 uncensored observations

Note how the sign of the union coefficient changes sign and becomes insignificant as we increase the truncation level. One possible explanation is that unions primarily have a positive effect on wages for workers at the low end of the income distribution. When we truncate these low income workers from our sample, the union effect disappears. This can also explain the larger effect of education for the truncated sample.

- NOTES -

- NOTES -

- NOTES -

- NOTES -

- NOTES -